LANDSCAPING
WITH
CONTAINER
PLANTS

Landscaping with Container Plants

JIM WILSON

HOUGHTON MIFFLIN COMPANY

Boston   1990

. . . .

Frontispiece: An elegant dooryard planting shows the advantages of different elevations. The taller ten-gallon tubs of tulips and pansies stand above two-gallon containers of white and purple violas.

PHOTO BY JOHN NEUBAUER

*For information about permission to reproduce selections
from this book, write to Permissions, Houghton Mifflin
Company, 2 Park Street, Boston, Massachusetts 02108.*

*Library of Congress Cataloging-in-Publication Data
Wilson, James W. (James Wesley), date.
Landscaping with container plants / Jim Wilson.
p.   cm.
ISBN 0-395-49864-3
1. Container gardening.   2. Landscape gardening.   I. Title.
SB418.W53   1990   89-39866
635.9'86—dc20   CIP*

Printed in the United States of America

Book design by Kathleen Westray

BOMC offers recordings and compact discs, cassettes
and records. For information and catalog write to
BOMR, Camp Hill, PA 17012.

TO MY WIFE, JANE

Contents

Still, it's safe to assume that this early form of container gardening was not widely practiced. Even many hundreds of years later, when ordinary people cultivated plants for their own pleasure, container gardening was pretty much restricted to the occasional flowerpot or windowbox. Not until late in the twentieth century — in fact, not until now — could it be described as a distinct and important branch of home horticulture.

The timing is due partly to an irony and partly to technology. The irony is that just when gardening has become one of the most popular forms of recreation in the United States, many Americans are finding themselves with little or no land on which to garden. As more and more of us live in towns and cities, in condominiums, high-rise apartment buildings, or new houses built on tiny plots, the big back yard has been replaced by a deck, a patio, a terrace, or a balcony. In older suburbs, where houses were built on generous amounts of land, the landscapes have matured, and the major form of gardening they call for is maintenance.

The answer, of course, is to grow plants in containers — to create a landscape with container plants. Here is where technology comes in, for if you had tried to grow a container garden thirty or forty years ago, you would probably have given up in discouragement as your plants succumbed to root diseases, waterlogged soil, or, conversely, soil that dried out too quickly. The situation was like that facing the inventors of powered aircraft: workable airframes existed before the Wright brothers took off at Kitty Hawk, but the progress of aeronautics was delayed to a large degree by the lack of a lightweight, high-performance engine that could make flight dependable.

Lightweight, high-performance artificial soil is the technological development that has made container gardening dependable. Beyond that, the new slow-release fertilizers and the even newer surfactants and polymers, which reduce the frequency of watering, make it possible today to grow plants in containers as easily, predictably, and successfully as in a garden. Finally, as homeowners turn to containers for their gardening pleasure, they find that nurseries and garden centers now offer hundreds of dwarf and miniature varieties of plants suitable for growing in restricted spaces, as well as a wonderfully wide variety of containers in which to grow them.

Gardening in containers has some drawbacks — there is a smaller margin

for error, so you must pay close attention to the condition of the plants, because everything they need has to come from you — but it has many advantages. It's neat: you can get your hands into the soil without muddying your feet, and if you don't like to bend down, you can elevate your garden. It's efficient: artificial soil warms up more quickly, can be planted earlier, and produces earlier crops than garden soil. But for me, the greatest boon of all is liberation from weeding. Container soils are virtually free of weed seeds. A few may blow in or be tracked in by birds with dirty feet, but pulling the occasional weed out of artificial soil is so easy that the revenge factor is completely missing.

Gardening in containers is worlds removed from growing plants in the ground. It isn't easier, nor is it harder, but it calls on the gardener to master a whole new set of rules. I hope this book will both inspire you to look at the exterior of your home with an eye to landscaping with container plants and show you how to do it. You will find that a few well-chosen plants in a few well-placed containers make a greater visual impact in your garden than a whole new bed of flowers.

. . . .

Half-round baskets make charming planters against a door or a wall. This basket of petunias, ivy-leaved geraniums, and trailing vinca decorates the door of the Victory Garden's toolshed at Lexington Gardens.

PHOTO BY JIM WILSON

I

⚜

DESIGNING WITH CONTAINER PLANTS

This beautiful stairway was created by moving the stair rail
eighteen inches in from the ends of the steps so that the potted
plants could be set out of the way of foot traffic.

PHOTO BY JOANNE PAVIA

CHAPTER I

Gardening Where There Is No Soil

Plants in containers enable you to transform almost any hard surface into a living landscape. Wherever you can place pots or hang baskets, you can have a garden — on a deck, a patio, a paved courtyard, an outdoor staircase, a balcony, a terrace, or a rooftop. The garden you design will depend on the size of the area and your pocketbook, the part of the country in which you live, the amount of time you want to

Bougainvillea beautifies a blank wall, and containers of annuals in half barrels and redwood tubs complete the picture.

PHOTO BY DEREK FELL

spend gardening, the degree and duration of sunlight your plants will receive, and, above all, your own tastes and needs. Nevertheless, some special considerations apply to any container garden.

Size and Position

Scale is one of the first things you should think about. Your plants should be in scale with the site. Unfortunately, in most gardens they are not. It is hard to find a container or plant so large that it visually overpowers its location. Too often the problem lies with insignificant containers that get lost against a busy or conflicting background. One easy solution is to group small pots inside a larger container.

Poor position can also be a shortcoming. It is usually the result of placing containers too low. A variety of levels is desirable; at least some of your plants should be at waist height or higher. Good positioning is a matter of safety, too. You don't want to put your planters where they will knock people's heads, but you have to protect heavy containers on pedestals, benches, and tables from rambunctious pets, active children, careless visitors, and high winds. Tall pedestals should have a firm, wide stance, and their tops should be broad enough to hold a container steady if they are nudged. Tables and benches should be level and set on a firm base. Wire cages should be free of projecting barbs that might snag passersby. Above all, hooks for hanging baskets should be replaced whenever possible with bolts that go clear through the supporting timber. Suspend hanging baskets either at chest level, where people can see them, or more than six feet high, where only basketball players will bump them.

Another consideration when you are gardening in containers on a hard surface is rain. Light rains are lovely; heavy ones can be a disaster, unless you have taken precautions. Although the number and size of drainage holes in your planters may be adequate for hand watering, just imagine what happens during a torrential rain. The headspace below the rim of the container fills up and overflows again and again. Particles of light material such as bark and perlite float to the top and spill over. After the rain, the patio or balcony is a mess, and you have to top off the soil in the containers. To avoid these problems, leave extra headspace in the containers when you pot

In this well-designed courtyard garden, cinerarias in ten-gallon basins brighten the greenery of conifers and ivy in large ceramic containers.

PHOTO BY LINDA YANG

your plants, then mulch with shredded hardwood bark, which tends to form a mat that keeps particles of mix from floating, or with decorative stones if you garden in a cool climate.

If you garden above the ground on a terrace, a balcony, or a rooftop, especially in a building you do not own outright, you should consider some other factors. The two most important are weight and water. Weight can accumulate very quickly in a container garden; for example, a single planter measuring twelve inches on each side and holding a cubic foot of planter mix can weigh about fifty pounds when wet. A twenty-five-gallon container the size of a large garbage can can weigh two hundred pounds when filled with moist planter mix containing sand.

Clearly, your first step should be to use ultra-light artificial soil (see Chapter 6). Equally important where weight is a problem is the way you place your containers. Instead of grouping them together, space them in a line along the walls of the roof or balcony, pulled in about twelve inches to avoid stressing the metal flashing between the surrounding wall and the roof. Don't even think about building a stationary planter against a roof wall, the weight of the wet planter mix can pull the flashing loose, and then every time it rains or you water your garden, water can run down the wall beneath the protective membrane and spread out over the ceiling below.

Decks, too, are subject to overloading from heavy containers. You can minimize downwarping of timbers by positioning heavy containers or groups of smaller containers over or near supporting posts. Where aesthetics are secondary, you might want to spread out the weight of large containers by setting them on pallets, which are often available at modest cost at company shipping docks. A typical pallet will spread the load of a container over sixteen square feet and is especially handy for elevating several small pots or planters.

Access to water is relatively easy to arrange if you have your own balcony, terrace, or penthouse. Unless you install an automatic irrigation system with an emitter in each container, you'll want a faucet near the plants, so you

Weight and Water

❧

Enjoy this little garden from indoors or on the deck. It is perfectly suited to the modern architecture of the house.
PHOTO BY DON NORMARK

Imagine how austere this entrance would
be without the geraniums in matched
pots and wrought-iron planters.
PHOTO BY GEORGE TALOUMIS

don't have to drag a hose through your apartment. If your garden is of significant size, a watering can is not likely to be adequate.

On terraces and rooftops, excess water enters the drains provided for rainwater; neighbors below you hardly ever know when you are watering, unless you overshoot with the spray. However, balconies with floors that have a slight grade to shunt water off the front edge present a different situation. When the wind is toward your side of the building, drainage water can blow into balconies below you. The considerate gardener waters early in the morning, when most folks are indoors. Watering at night is not a good idea, because leaves that are wet all night are prone to fungal diseases.

Just as most city people don't live in penthouses, most rooftop gardens are not luxury landscapes. They are more likely to be found atop old apartment buildings, row houses, or commercial buildings that have been converted to housing. Residents use the rooftops for sunning, exercising, drying clothes, entertaining, and gardening, just as suburbanites use their decks and back yards for these activities. In general, these areas are sloped just enough to keep rainwater from collecting and causing leaks, and are tarred, sometimes with a crushed-rock topping. Some rooftops hold up well under weight; some don't.

Building managers and absentee owners generally go along with occupants' use of the roof for gardening — until weight stress and drainage water cause leaks or cracks in apartment ceilings. Then they tighten the rules, lock the doors to the roof, and make it hard on all the residents. So it behooves urban gardeners to avoid causing leaks and structural damage by spreading out the weight of containers.

Watering rooftop gardens if no faucet is handy is an exercise in ingenuity. One season of lugging buckets up flights of stairs is enough to blight anyone's gardening instincts. The solution is often to attach an adapter to an apartment faucet, thread a water hose to it, and unroll the hose as you work your way upstairs. The new lightweight "lay flat" hoses are a great improvement on the old-fashioned kind, but you still have to work out a signal so someone downstairs can turn the water on and off. If you attach an on-off valve to the hose and turn the water on before you leave the apartment, the heavy, water-laden, dripping hose is a pain to lug to the roof. If you go out your front door, you leave your apartment vulnerable, even if you set the

Urban imagination! At the foot of
Boston's Beacon Hill, a grape-stake
palisade is draped with ivy and topped
with windowboxes of vivid geraniums.

PHOTO BY GEORGE TALOUMIS

The rooftop garden above, in Manhattan's Soho district, is a center
for informal entertaining. Taking care of the assortment of trees,
shrubs, flowers, and herbs is made easy by the hose outlet
on the left.
Right: On the upper terrace of John and Gwen Burgee's
Manhattan penthouse, irises, roses, baby's-breath, and other
perennials bloom in the protection of a black pine tree.
PHOTOS BY PETER C. JONES

catch chain and crack the door. Out the window and up the fire escape is a better route than the stairs for the young, athletic, and daring, and you can leave the hose in place from day to day. If you have a building superintendent, your best bet might be a substantial Christmas gift and a broad hint that a water faucet and hose on the roof would be a valuable adjunct to the building's fire-protection program.

Gardeners who have never lived in a high-rise building have to stretch their minds to imagine the difficulties associated with terrace, balcony, and rooftop gardening in an urban environment. But the plus side of lofty gardens is the extraordinary pleasure they give their creators, who choose their plants with great care, enjoy them at every stage of growth, fuss over them, and use them in many ways. Plants fill the human need for a link with nature and a sanctuary from the stress of urban life. City gardeners also enjoy an unexpected bonus from their congested environment: urban warmth moderates temperatures enough to minimize the loss of perennials and woody plants to winter cold.

Perhaps the most rewarding part of the job of hauling supplies, containers, and plants to a rooftop to put together a container garden is the understanding looks and comments you get. So many people are gardening in containers that your neighbors will recognize the signs. A bag of planter mix over your shoulder or a strawberry jar in your arms marks you as one of the fellowship. You care enough about plants to turn the work of preparation into an adventure, and you are not about to let the lack of soil deter you from growing!

The Plus Side of Urban Container Gardening

An airy summer scene at John and Gwen Burgee's two-story penthouse. The lattice arbor designed by John, an architect, is flanked by planters of honey locust trees, flowering shrubs, and silver artemesia. A pool and a fountain add a tranquil touch to this home above the Manhattan streets.

PHOTO BY PETER C. JONES

CHAPTER 2

Containers in the Landscape

CONTAINER GAR-
dening is not the exclusive province of landless
town or city gardeners. Although its appeal to
those who have ground is less obvious, there
are any number of situations in which containers can solve practical or design dilemmas —
to say nothing of the dilemma of the avid gardener who doesn't have room for another bed
or border.

Of all the gardens I've grown in my lifetime,

No gold rush here—three old mining carts are parked on a
lawn and planted with tulips and forget-me-nots, a
delightful way to bring color to an all-green landscape.

PHOTO BY JERRY PAVIA

[17]

the only one that really satisfied me was a garden I designed and built from scratch. But even with that one I was like a discontented homemaker, forever changing beds and plantings to reflect my evolving taste in landscaping. It was harder work than rearranging furniture, and often the effects weren't evident for a year or more. Today when I want to change my garden, I am more likely to create new islands of interest with container plants.

Gardeners who have lived in the same house for many years commonly complain that areas that once got enough sunlight to grow vegetables are now shaded by trees, which have grown up so that none of the property receives enough sun to produce a crop. These gardeners, too, are resorting to planters, which they can move to follow the sun. Homegrown tomatoes are worth the trouble.

Containers are also a good solution to the problem of poor soil. If your home is built on rock, deep sand, or hardpan clay, improving the soil can be a difficult, expensive, long-term project. Avid gardeners enjoy overcoming these obstacles and take understandable pride in achieving the kind of fertile, porous loam that grows good plants. However, for working people who haven't the time for such intensive gardening — and for those who haven't the interest — the solution is to buy artificial soil, which is perfectly formulated to grow plants in containers. This isn't exactly instant gratification, but it comes close.

The typical suburban front yard of grass and foundation shrubs is neither colorful nor interesting. Without tearing up the shrubs, you can make an attractive little dooryard garden by clustering a group of flowers in large containers on each side of the entrance. You can do the same at a front gate. Unlike a "real" garden, which has its ups and downs as flowers bloom and fade, a container garden can always be at its peak, if you simply replace old plants with young ones you have had on hold elsewhere.

Windowboxes make any house look pretty. We Americans don't use them nearly as much as we could, but I suspect that is going to change. As I write this, the television show *The Victory Garden* is selecting the winners of its annual contest. For the first time, the subject of the contest is not vegetable and flower gardens but windowboxes and other containers.

If container plants can decorate a house, they can also camouflage an eyesore. Try putting a collection of hanging baskets at various heights

"Lift up thine eyes": a planter box above an ornamental gate is festooned with geraniums, petunias, and lobelias.

PHOTO BY JOANNE PAVIA

"Welcome to my garden": Terra-cotta
pots of wax begonias, lobelias,
geraniums, and petunias flank the gate of
garden writer George Taloumis.

PHOTO BY GEORGE TALOUMIS

Mary Higgins with the windowbox that
won her the first prize in the 1989 *Victory
Garden* container contest.

PHOTO BY TY GREENLEES

against a blank garage wall or back fence; fill them with trailing vines as well
as flowers. You can also use hanging baskets to help correct one of the most
common landscaping problems, the dreary flat garden devoid of changes in
elevation.

Kitchen Gardens

Every garden needs a few intimate areas that arouse pleasant feelings —
serenity, oneness with nature, or simply satisfaction with your handi-
work. Kitchen gardens can also gratify a more fundamental need, by provid-
ing convenient access to herbs, salad greens, patio tomatoes, and dwarf
varieties of other vegetables, all of which thrive in containers.

Make your kitchen garden quickly accessible from the kitchen. If that
sounds like an amazing revelation of the obvious, think of the many food
gardens planted at the back of the yard. In rain or hot sun, the few extra
feet you have to walk are enough to make you reach for dried herbs instead

of harvesting fresh condiments, or use insipid shipped-in lettuce instead of picking some fresh leaf lettuce. If you have room for only a small garden near the kitchen, fill the space with containers planted with the salad vegetables and herbs you use often.

You can pack a wide variety of vegetables and herbs into a small space by setting containers at various heights or by stairstepping them. The neatest kitchen gardens I've seen consist of large-diameter flue tiles of different lengths stacked from knee to waist height and filled with planter mix. You can also buy pyramid planters, which enable you to grow more in a small area. Or you can collect benches and tables, or stack blocks or plastic crates to various heights and set containers on them.

Cabbages, violas, and white sweet Williams in a half barrel on a bark-covered path at Victory Garden South, at Callaway Gardens in Pine Mountain, Georgia.

PHOTO BY JOANNE PAVIA

A series of white-stained redwood planters soften a privacy wall on a beautifully landscaped deck. The tallest planter is lined with stainless steel to make a pool. A small recirculating pump and six copper dishes (three on the wall and three in the pool) make a pleasant little waterfall. The planter to the left of the pool has an espaliered bristlecone pine; the vine to the right was a volunteer seedling that struck the owners' fancy.

PHOTO BY GAY BUMGARNER, PHOTO/NATS

An old claw-foot bathtub from a remodeled Victorian farmhouse in
Virginia is a contained pond for hardy water lilies, dwarf papyrus,
dwarf bamboo, and sagittaria.

PHOTO BY DIANE RELF

The folks who grow and sell water plants, fish, pool liners, and accessories tell me that water gardening is catching on and that people are growing water plants in tubs, barrels, urns, and other containers. A little epoxy glue and a plastic plug can even convert a large terra-cotta pot with a hole in the bottom to a fishpond.

Small cultivars of water lilies and other aquatic plants will thrive in large containers of still water, but the water can become a bit stale for fish. However, by combining attractive containers at various levels and interconnecting them so that the water can descend from one to another, you can keep the water moving, recirculating it with a small pump and filtering it to keep it cooler. A fountain will contribute the soothing sound of water to the garden environment and will attract birds. Put your water lilies in a container of relatively still water, though, to ensure flowering.

In most areas, you should construct container water gardens for easy dismantling when cold weather arrives, or equip them with a small heater. Freezing and thawing can destroy containers and kill the plants and fish. If you design for quick assembly, dismantling should also go quickly. You can nest and store containers, pumps, filters, and plants, and keep your small goldfish in fishbowls indoors.

The next time you walk around your garden, let your imagination be your guide. Start with one area and a single project — an herb garden, a window-box, a collection of pots at the front door, or simply one big container of spring bulbs beside a garden seat (you can add a new container every year). Whether you garden for the pleasure of growing plants or to create something beautiful — or both, as most of us do — I think you'll find that container gardening adds a new dimension to your enjoyment as well as your environment.

Water Gardens

Ready-Made Containers

A "stone" trough made of concrete and vermiculite is lightweight and drains well. A steel mesh core gives it strength. Note the careful choice of alpines and dwarf conifers.

PHOTO BY JOHN NEUBAUER

Terra-cotta planters are the most "natural-looking" ones you can buy, but they are rather fragile. Rough handling can chip or crack them, and freezing and thawing can destroy them entirely. Still, many sizes and shapes are available: standard pots, baskets with handles, strawberry jars, basins, molded farm animals and pets, and stylish planter boxes. The natural color of red clay lightens with exposure to the sun. Occasionally you can find containers fired from white clay, which are quite handsome.

Concrete containers range from somewhat crudely cast pieces to smooth, symmetrical creations that a landscape architect might choose. Some resemble oversize pots; others mimic urns, jardinières, or baskets festooned with vines; still others are fan-shaped, cylindrical, square, or rectangular. Concrete containers are only slightly more expensive than terra-cotta ones and are vastly more durable. I know of some that have withstood Zone 7 winters for twenty years with no sign of deterioration. (A map of climate zones in the United States appears at the end of the appendix.)

A concrete bowl washed with aqua paint sets off a dozen pansy
plants making faces at passers-by.

PHOTO BY GEORGE TALOUMIS

For contemporary shapes, look to the thin-walled containers made of a blend of fiberglass and concrete. They are as durable as concrete and considerably lighter, which is a great advantage where weight is a consideration. The blends have a smooth finish without the bubbles or lumps often seen in cast-concrete articles. To me, the tall cylinders and wide, shallow basins of concrete and fiberglass are most appealing.

All-fiberglass containers are even lighter in weight and are reasonably durable — perhaps the strongest planters for their weight. The better-made ones look good in modern settings but are a bit too slick for naturalistic or rustic gardens. Most are designed for interior use but will hold up if used outdoors.

Molded or injected plastic containers have the advantage of being inexpensive as well as lightweight. The heavier and somewhat flexible buckets and tubs hold up better than the thin stiff pots, which can shatter, especially when exposed to extreme cold. They come in several colors, the basic ones being brown, black, green, and white. White absorbs the least heat; plants grown in them suffer less root damage from intense summer heat caused by direct sunlight. You can group plastic containers of vegetables and herbs so that the plants hide most of the pots.

Naturally rot-resistant wooden tubs and boxes are made from California redwood, cedar, or southern cypress. Wood is the preferred material for windowboxes, because it insulates the soil from solar heat and has a natural texture, and it is worth the extra cost. If you empty and store wooden containers at the end of each growing season, they should last for three to five years in the South, longer in the North. Common pine or fir is often painted to resemble redwood, but it won't hold up nearly as well.

You may occasionally see large planter boxes made of treated wood. The problem with most of these is that the wood is poorly cured and tends to warp or twist when exposed to the sun. Treated wood soon loses its green color, and it doesn't take well to painting. Nevertheless, acceptable treated wood containers are sold at relatively low prices. If you can find wooden apple baskets of green-stained treated wood, in half-bushel or bushel sizes, buy them for containers. They hold up well, drain readily, don't blow over, look good, and have handy wire handles. Nurserymen used them for years before plastic containers became available.

This redwood bench surrounded by planters and topped by a slatted arbor was designed for the Victory Garden.

PHOTO BY GARY MOTTAU

Callaway Gardens in Pine Mountain,
Georgia, is the home of Victory Garden
South. Here is one of our container
plantings—pansies and lobelias in flue
tiles of varying heights.

PHOTO BY JOANNE PAVIA

Molded containers, made from wood fiber, a renewable resource, look good, cost relatively little, and are environmentally responsible. I like the smaller ones, from about one-bushel capacity down, because you can pick them up from the bottom. The fiber is pressed into a wood texture and absorbs so little water that the pot stays rigid throughout all or most of the growing season. Some of these containers are dipped in wax for extra life, but the process darkens the fiber and imparts an artificial look.

Because no base metal except lead can withstand the corrosive action of fertilizer salts, and because of high heat conductivity, sheet-metal containers are not satisfactory for outdoor use. Lead or faux-lead cast-aluminum alloy containers, which are usually copies of antique objects, are available from specialty suppliers.

Wire hanging baskets are superior to plastic ones because of their strength; they can take a beating from high winds. Baskets up to twenty-four inches in diameter are available from mail-order sources and in well-stocked garden centers; those already lined with long-fiber sphagnum peat moss cost about 50 percent more than the basket alone. You can also order molded fiber or burlap liners for hanging baskets. These don't insulate plant roots as well as the thick mat of sphagnum moss, but they are easier and faster to work with. Baskets are usually shipped with tripod-type hangers twisted into a hook. You can also buy wire half-baskets that hang flush against a wall or fence.

Adapted Containers

I never cease to marvel at the excellent containers people make out of scrounged crates, wooden boxes, and other "found" items. Apple and citrus crates, made of thin wood and wire and lined with plastic, will hold two or three gallons of planter mix, and sometimes more. Wooden fish crates are too malodorous to attract most scroungers, but they work just fine for growing vegetables after they have been washed with ammonia.

Innovative gardeners convert all sorts of receptacles into containers for plants: sections of concrete culverts, chimney flue tiles, terra-cotta drainage tiles, sinks, bathtubs, crates, ammunition boxes (swords into plowshares!), cylinders of wire fencing, and so on, *ad infinitum*. Planters that can stay

Hanging moss-based dish gardens swing
from a wrought-iron tree. Driftwood
and seashells set off the miniature
flowering plants.

PHOTO BY THOMAS E. ELTZROTH

In Maine, a driftwood "canoe" floats on a lawn-grass sea with a
cargo of red and white petunias.

PHOTO BY GEORGE TALOUMIS

A planted post diverts the eye from a
utilitarian graveled corner. The baskets
are lined with moss.

PHOTO BY THOMAS E. ELTZROTH

. . . .

Silvery dusty miller cools down the
bright color of the ice plant
(*Mesembryanthemum crystallinum*)
in a redwood container.

PHOTO BY GARY MOTTAU

plants. The majority of terra-cotta, concrete, plastic, and fiber pots for sale in garden centers are in this size range. Compact annual flowers, salad vegetables, miniature roses, perennials, cacti, and succulents are just a few of the plants that will grow well in them. The largest hanging baskets will hold three to five gallons of mix. I wouldn't fool with smaller hanging baskets, because they dry out too rapidly. Most windowboxes are in this size range too, primarily because larger ones are too difficult to handle and to support, and smaller ones are prone to dry out.

Fast-growing plants can double or quadruple in size in one growing season. They need containers that appear too big at planting time but that will just about equal in volume the size of the top growth at maturity. The most versatile containers for compact annual flowers, strawberries, standard roses, and small vegetables are in the seven- to ten-gallon range. At this size, short, rather wide containers work better than tall, narrow ones. The tall ones drain faster than necessary. Short, squatty ones, even if they have six or eight drainage holes in the bottom, hold water a little longer, which gives large plants an opportunity to drink fully before the excess water drains away. A typical short container in this class measures about nine inches high and eighteen inches across; it holds just under ten gallons of planter mix.

It is sometimes hard to find ready-made containers that are large enough to hold fast-growing, robust flowers, vegetables, and dwarf trees. Vigorous annuals will completely fill the soil with a mass of roots by the end of the growing season, and at maturity they will be at least a hundred times as large as they were as seedlings. Dwarf or compact trees don't grow as fast, of course, and can live with a certain degree of root crowding.

Only a few ready-made options are available in the ten- to thirty-gallon range: plastic garbage cans, half whiskey barrels, thick plastic chemical drums (neutralized and washed thoroughly), short segments of concrete culvert, large cast-concrete containers, and flue tiles. You can make rustic containers of this size from treated lumber. If the box is to hold fruit trees or vegetable plants, line it with plastic, punched for drainage, to keep the roots from contact with the chemical wood preservatives.

Here's a bit of advice for gardeners in Zones 7, 8, and 9 — the Deep South and warm West. For sunny sites, avoid dark-colored containers, which absorb more heat than white or light-hued ones. I have visited nur-

site, alone or in a group? (Before going further, I look closely at the preliminary choices to see whether they have drainage holes. Some pots are designed without a hole so water cannot drain onto the surroundings. With these, you have to plant in a smaller pot, which you set inside the larger container on blocks, to raise it above any water that might accumulate in the bottom. Trapped drainage water stagnates if it is not emptied weekly.)

Another factor I consider when selecting containers is whether the plant or plants to be potted up are slow-growing or relatively fast-growing. The slowest of all woody plants are the dwarf conifers, followed by cacti and succulents, broad-leaved evergreens, citrus plants, flowering shrubs, roses, and fruit trees, and then perennial flowers, annuals, and vegetables. Very slow-growing plants increase in size by only 10 percent or so each year. With these, you can start with a container that would just about hold the top growth if you stuffed it in. (I'm not recommending that you plant your plants upside down; I'm just giving you a volumetric comparison.) Small, very slow-growing plants should not be overpotted — planted in large containers on the assumption that they will grow to fill them. That's like fitting children with shoes two sizes bigger than they need. Overpotted slow-growing plants can contract root rot from water retained in the extra soil.

Moderately slow-growing plants increase in size by about 25 to 50 percent each year. Containers for these should be about one and a half times the size of the mature top growth. There's no need to try for an exact match between a fast-growing plant and container size; just buy the largest you can afford, since the plant will grow to fit it.

Realistically, one-gallon containers are about the smallest practical size for outdoor planting. Although they are the right size to support a slow-growing plant through a season, they do dry out rapidly and tend to blow over. Experienced gardeners group three to five such pots in a large, shallow container and fill in around them with ropy sphagnum moss weighted down with stones. The filler prevents the pots from blowing over and drying out, but does not keep them too wet. You should lift the pots every two or three weeks and trim off the protruding roots, so that when it comes time to shift the plants to larger pots, you will not shock them into losing leaves by pruning off long, heavy roots.

Three- to five-gallon containers are good for moderately slow-growing

Windowboxes of a somewhat greater depth than the front-to-back dimension look best; a box thirty-six inches long, sixteen inches deep, and twelve to fourteen inches front-to-back is as large as most people can handle and will span the average window. Insert a sheet of Styrofoam on the side exposed to afternoon sun to keep the soil cooler. Drill two rows of three-quarter-inch drainage holes in the bottom board.

You can make great-looking lightweight fake stone sinks by combining cement, vermiculite or perlite, and perhaps sphagnum peat moss for a rustic look. Experiment with various combinations on a small scale first, by pouring a little of the compound into the bottom of a plastic pot, setting a slightly smaller pot inside it, and stuffing more compound into the cavity between the two pots. After three or four hours, twist out the inner pot and invert and tap out the still-moist compound pot. Let it dry, then make corrections in the mixture and upscale the amount to make a stone sink. Cement should make up one quarter to one third of the compound by volume. One formula that works is one part cement, one part sand, and two parts sphagnum peat moss.

Typically, fake stone sinks are two to two and a half feet long, fourteen to eighteen inches deep, and about twelve inches wide. The walls are quite thick, in keeping with the originals, which were chipped out of granite. Use two windowboxes, one smaller than the other, as the inner and outer molds, or two large basins of different sizes. Oil the wood before casting so the compound won't stick to it. Make the compound rather stiff, trowel a bottom layer into the larger mold, set the smaller mold on top, trowel more compound down the sides, then ram it down with a stick to eliminate airholes. Drill six or eight drainage holes in the finished container. These lightweight planters age attractively and have good insulating properties.

Choosing the Right Containers

❦

The first thing I consider when selecting containers is the site. Does it call for a single freestanding container or a group of pots set at different heights? What about a hanging basket or a flat-backed wire container that can be hung from a wall like a windowbox? Within the portable size range of three to thirty gallons, which size, shape, and color will look best at the

where you place them don't need bottoms; they work best if you put down a layer of landscape cloth before you set them on the ground, to prevent tree roots from growing up into them. Cylinders of wire-mesh fencing can be lined with plastic or burlap to hold planter mix. Containers with no holes can be drilled for drainage. Stone is no barrier; use a masonry bit.

Humorous or campy containers are personal expressions that may appeal more to you than to visitors. For universal appeal, convert an old birdhouse into a hanging basket, fill a stone sink or a cracked kettle with flowers, or grow salad greens in an old horse trough or a wooden bushel basket. I remember clearly an abandoned rowboat filled with marigolds and an eagle-claw bathtub gleaming with water lilies that I saw years ago.

If a container has drainage holes, won't rot (or can be protected with plastic), and will hold at least a gallon of planter mix, you can grow things in it. Driftwood, hollowed-out pumice, tree stumps with hollow centers, old work shoes, and joints of giant bamboo all work well. Just walk around your yard and you may see half-a-dozen nonfunctioning items that you can stuff with soil and plant. If the cavity is too leaky to hold soil, set a potted plant in it and fill in around it with ropy green sphagnum moss. Put it where you won't forget to water it regularly and *voilà* — an instant *objet d'art*.

Home-constructed containers are usually of three types: windowboxes, freestanding containers, or lightweight pseudo stone sinks or basins made of concrete blended with vermiculite or perlite.

Any handyman can measure, saw, and put together a windowbox or planter, but let me caution you to strengthen it with corner cleats and assemble it with sturdy screws. Moist planter mix is heavy, and wood tends to swell and shrink. Nails won't hold for long. Set the box on sturdy wooden brackets sawed from treated two-by-four lumber screwed together and mounted to wall studs with lag screws. On brick walls, tap lead anchors into holes bored with a masonry bit. The top edge of the box should be level with or slightly below the window, so it won't block light.

Windowboxes should be portable when filled with planter mix; you will need to take them down and dump the contents at the end of the season.

Do-It-Yourself Planters

series where the outer row of black containers in a block, particularly those on the southern and western sides, held plants that were not growing as well as those in pots shaded by adjacent containers. I knocked out the root balls and could clearly see that excessive heat on the exposed side had killed all the roots within an inch of the pot wall. In semidesert or semitropical situations, you might have to site containers so that shade from walls or other structures falls over them from midafternoon on.

You can find a good selection of containers at large retail nurseries or garden centers, at mass pottery outlets, or at roadside stands that either sell their own concrete planters or distribute containers for manufacturers. Mail-order specialists offer designer containers that can rarely be found in retail establishments. Large garden centers serving an affluent clientele carry large containers in many designs and materials — wood, plastic, stone, fiberglass, and wood fiber — and offer the option of preplanted containers. These are generally of three types: freestanding planters and hanging baskets closely planted with blooming annuals and vines, containers of tropical and foliage plants for shady corners, and dramatic plantings of succulents, cacti, yuccas, and other drought-resistant plants for hot, dry areas. Large preplanted containers can be formidably heavy, so ask the nursery to deliver them and set them in place; the plants should be protected from drying winds during transport.

As the trend toward container gardening grows, the mixture of cultivars in planted containers is becoming more imaginative and eclectic. Of all the nurseries in the country, Rogers Garden Center, just uphill from Newport Beach, California, has the most fantastic collection of planted containers. On the East Coast, Behnke Nurseries, in Beltsville, Maryland, has a marvelous collection of planters, compatible plants, and planted containers. In the South, Tallahassee Nurseries caters to container gardeners, and in New England, Lexington Gardens at Lexington, Massachusetts, displays planted containers in its demonstration garden (where host Bob Thomson introduces *The Victory Garden*).

I love shopping for containers at the large pottery outlets, such as Williamsburg (Virginia) Pottery, Craven Pottery in north Georgia (where the native red clay is used to make terra-cotta planters of many sizes), and Waccamaw Pottery in the Carolinas. These places display a huge inventory

Mailbox planters make even a delivery of junk mail palatable. The box on this page, photographed in July, features geraniums, lobelias, petunias, and variegated gill-over-the-ground. The October mailbox, opposite, has a seasonal display of mums.

PHOTOS BY GEORGE TALOUMIS

CONTAINER SIZES
■ ■ ■

Containers are labeled either by capacity in gallons or, in the case of pots, by diameter in inches. Neither unit of measurement is particularly helpful, because potting soils and planter mixes are often sold by the cubic foot or by weight, and the weight of artificial soil depends not only on its density but on the moisture content. To determine how much planter mix you need to fill your containers, use these conversion factors:

$$\text{1 gallon} = \text{231 cubic inches}$$
$$\text{1728 cubic inches} = \text{1 cubic foot}$$

Thus, a one-cubic-foot bag of planter mix will fill about seven one-gallon containers.

Figuring the capacity of cylindrical or square containers goes quickly if you use a calculator: simply multiply the area of the top times the height. For example, to figure the capacity of a six-inch-high cylinder with an interior diameter of seven inches, use the high school formula of $\pi r^2 \times h$, or $3.14 \times 12.25 \times 6$. It comes out to almost exactly 231 cubic inches, or one gallon.

Figuring the capacity of a tapered pot is slightly more difficult. You have to average the surface area of the top and bottom, then multiply by the height (or length).

Sparkling with dew and trailing ivy, this Victorian urn is filled with bright annuals and topped with a handsome foliage houseplant.

PHOTO BY JOHN NEUBAUER

of terra-cotta, fiberglass, and concrete pots in large sizes. Their large, shallow basins and capacious strawberry jars practically beg to be taken home and planted. They also offer a saucer for every size pot. Although you don't need saucers for outdoor container plants, because drainage water can stand in them and set the stage for root rot, you can invert them to use as pedestals.

When you drive by roadside markets of terra-cotta and concrete containers, you may be put off by some of the dreadful accessories they sell as well. Cherubs, goddesses, clusters of grapes, sheaves of wheat, baskets of fruit, serpentine vines, little boys from Brussels plumbed to tinkle a stream of water, frogs, dwarfs, nymphs, leprechauns, dolphins, toadstools, ducks and geese, windmills . . . they have whatever turns you on, or off. Close your eyes to these and concentrate on the containers, benches, tables, and pedestals. Concrete looks raw and new, but it will quickly take on a patina if you paint it a few times with manure tea or buttermilk. Generally, the simpler and cleaner the design of the pot, the more compatible it will be with a wide range of plants.

Durability of containers goes hand in hand with price. One-season, expendable containers are of course cheaper than heavy, solid containers that will last for years, perhaps for your gardening lifetime. You might want to start with temporary containers of plastic or pressed fiber, until you get the hang of growing. Then you can advance confidently to more expensive containers. When you invest $15 to $100 in a capacious container, you need to think of it as a garden ornament that can come to life when planted.

II

❦

CHOICE PLANTS
FOR CONTAINER
GARDENS

A handsome splash of color on the edge of a deck near the water.

CHAPTER 4

Ornamentals

V IRTUALLY ANY
form of flowering or foliage plant will be at
home in the container landscape — if you
choose the right species or variety, and if you
can provide the proper conditions for growth.
I have specifically selected the plants in this
section for growing in containers, but please
note that I have given hardiness zones, container sizes, and any other special requirements
for a particular plant where this information is

A striking display of tuberous and Rieger begonias at the
Strybing Arboretum in San Francisco.

PHOTO BY ANN REILLY, PHOTO/NATS

[5 3]

appropriate. All of these plants are good container choices, and should grow and show better than others in your garden.

Annuals

❦

F lowering annuals are the backbone of ornamental plantings in either freestanding or hanging containers. You can buy them in bloom and transplant them with little loss of momentum. They will give weeks, or even a season, of color at minimal cost.

To select the best annuals for containers, you need to know the growth habit of each plant, its range of colors, and its resistance to really hot weather and to frost. The list that follows includes my favorite container annuals. For your convenience, I have noted the following information for each kind:

- *Small, medium,* or *large*. This refers to the mature size of the plant. Small plants are less than twelve inches in height and spread; medium, eighteen to twenty-four inches; and large, ranging up from twenty-four inches.
- *Trailing, mounded,* or *erect* in form. Typically, people plant trailing annuals around the outside of the container, mounded ones near the center, and, in large freestanding containers, erect plants in the middle. Hanging baskets are usually planted with trailing and/or small mounded plants.
- *Cool-weather, heat-resistant,* or *very heat-resistant*. Where summers are long and hot, cool-weather flowers perform best if planted in late summer for fall and early winter color. Frost hardiness is noted.
- *Full-sun* or *shade-tolerant*. No flowering annuals will withstand more than moderate shade, and most prefer either full sun or light shade. "Shade-tolerant" means that the plant prefers full sun but will bloom in some shade.

Ageratum. Small, mounded to trailing, cool-weather, full-sun plants; will tolerate light shade in warm climates. Available in lavender, blue, pink, and white. Some cultivars mature at a height of six inches; others are taller. A frost-tender staple flower for edging large containers.

Marguerites, geraniums, and heliotropes in pots at the corner of this terrace meet the roses under the window to make a lovely summer garden.

Rudbeckias aren't fazed by summer heat.
Dwarf red salvia, moss rose, sweet
alyssum, and dwarf marigolds hide their
bare legs.

PHOTO BY THOMAS E. ELTZROTH

Asparagus fern. Tender perennial, usually grown as an annual. Medium, arching or mounded, very heat-resistant, shade-tolerant plants for hanging baskets or planters. Grown for the needlelike foliage; not a true fern. 'Myers' cultivar is best in hanging baskets, because it has plumy fronds.

Aster (dwarf types; the tall varieties are too lanky for containers). Medium, mounded, cool-weather, full-sun plants. 'Gem' grows to a height of ten inches, and is more practical and more durable than the ultra-dwarfs. Available in white, pink, rose, lavender, and purple. Will tolerate moderate frosts but is susceptible to aster yellows (see Chapter 11).

Australian drumstick flower (*Craspedia*). Medium, mounded, very heat-resistant, full-sun plants. New to American horticulture, this Australian native shoots up foot-high leafless stems topped with rounded, long-lasting yellow flowers. Foliage is silvery gray and grasslike.

Balsam (dwarf types). Medium, mounded, heat-resistant, shade-tolerant plants. Prefers full sun where summers are cool. Related to impatiens, but has larger leaves and flowers clustered in the axils of the main stems. 'Carambole', a dwarf, has violet, scarlet, white, and pink blossoms. Frost-tender.

Fancy-leaved begonia. Small to medium, mounded or trailing, moderately heat-resistant, shade-tolerant, frost-tender plants. Ordinarily grown as houseplants, fancy-leaved begonias make outstanding container specimens for shaded patios and for displays under trees, where they are protected from sun and wind. The large leaves dry out quickly and benefit from high humidity. Grown more for their colorful foliage than for flowers, some nevertheless have beautiful flower sprays.

Fibrous-rooted or **wax begonia.** Small, mounded, heat-resistant, moderately shade-tolerant, frost-tender plants. Prefers full sun except where summer temperatures often exceed 90°F. Very popular for its clean, shiny foliage and prolonged bloom. Choose the smaller-flowered types if you want small, dainty plants and the larger-flowered ones for medium-high plants. You can specify either green or bronze foliage. A wide color range is available: white, pink, rose, crimson, and scarlet.

Tuberous-rooted begonia. Medium, mounded or trailing, cool-weather, moderately shade-tolerant, frost-tender plants. On the West Coast and across the north to New England, a beautiful and choice container plant; unhappy in hot-summer areas. Trailing varieties for hanging baskets are available; 'Non-Stop Hybrid' is an erect type grown from seeds. Colors include white, most shades of red and pink, clear yellow, and orange.

Browallia. Medium, mounded to lax, moderately heat-resistant, moderately shade-tolerant plants. One of the best hanging-basket flowers if plants can be watered frequently. Mature plants hang gracefully. Available in blue, deep blue, and white. The ultra-dwarf 'Troll' variety remains compact. Not frost-hardy.

Brown-eyed Susan (*Rudbeckia*; dwarf). Small to medium, mounded, very heat-resistant, full-sun perennial usually grown as an annual. 'Goldilocks' has compact plants; taller cultivars are better suited to large planters.

Calendula (pot marigold). Medium, mounded, decidedly cool-weather, full-sun, frost-hardy plants. Stays very low and develops large flowers when winter-grown in mild climates. Elsewhere, seeds planted in spring will quickly become medium-tall plants with long flower stems and small flowers, in response to shortening nights. Available in bright yellow, gold, orange, and white, and, in the best dwarf cultivars such as 'Bon' or 'Fiesta Gitana', apricot as well. A cold-weather staple.

Candytuft (*Iberis umbellata*; dwarf). Small, mounded, cool-weather, full-sun, slightly frost-hardy plants. A showy old-fashioned flower for late spring bloom, with flat flower clusters like umbrellas. Available in many pastel shades plus dark red. 'Brilliant' stays small.

Carnation (dwarf). Small, mounded, cool-weather, full-sun, moderately frost-hardy plants. The tall cutting carnations are leggy and unkempt if not staked, so dwarf varieties are better for containers. Colors include white, pink, crimson, orange, and yellow with some picotee and penciling variations. 'Lilipot' remains compact at maturity. 'Fragrance' is taller and less double, but more fragrant.

Crested celosia (dwarf). Small, mounded, heat-resistant, full-sun, frost-tender plants. The curious flower crests resemble damask drapery or brain coral. Transplant when color is just showing, or earlier. Mulch to prevent soil from splashing onto the intricately folded crests. An extraordinary range of warm colors, including deep maroon, is available. Some varieties have bronze or purple foliage.

Plumed celosia (dwarf). Small, erect plants; like the crested celosia but more graceful and with spires. Best for the centers of large freestanding

Massive but cuddly 'Teddy Bear' dwarf
sunflowers look over the shoulders of
blue salvia and double yellow marigolds.
PHOTO BY THOMAS E. ELTZROTH

Protected from the afternoon sun,
hanging tuberous begonias overflow a
windowbox in a truly stunning display.

PHOTO BY THOMAS E. ELTZROTH

A perennial that does particularly well in
a pot is *Sedum spectabile*. The variety
pictured here is 'Brilliant'. The tall plant
to the right is *Canna* 'Maybelline'.

PHOTO BY GEORGE TALOUMIS

in an incredible assortment of sizes and colors and bicolors, including a dainty lavender-blue.

New Guinea impatiens. Medium, mounded, very heat-resistant, frost-tender, full-sun plants. This group of hybrids often sports brilliantly variegated leaves, larger than those of *I. wallerana*. Plants are more massive and durable. Prone to wilt in dry, windy areas exposed to full afternoon sun.

Lantana. Medium, mounded to trailing, very heat- and drought-resistant, full-sun, frost-tender plants. A perennial grown as an annual or wintered over indoors north of Zone 7. Withstands heat and drought that would kill other plants. Droops gracefully in hanging baskets or can be trained into a single-stem standard. 'Confetti' has multicolored flower sprays.

Lobelia. Small, mounded or trailing, moderately heat-resistant, full-sun, frost-tender plants. Grown for its unmatched blue and intense purple blooms against ferny foliage. The 'Pendula' and 'Cascade' series trail; other varieties are compact. Intolerant of prolonged heat and humidity.

Marigold. Small to medium, mounded to erect, heat-resistant, full-sun, frost-tender plants, near the top in popularity. The French and triploid types remain compact. The large-flowered African or 'Erecta' types grow erect. The small-flowered signet type is best for hanging baskets. Points to watch for in selecting marigold varieties: resistance to fading and blanking (aborted blossoms) in intense sun; ability to self-cover (new blooms and foliage hide spent blossoms); blooms that are fast-draining — that don't hold water and rot; and clarity of color.

Nasturtium. Medium, mounded to trailing, moderately heat-resistant, full-sun, frost-tender plants. The old 'Gleam' hybrids trail; the newer 'Jewel' types remain in mounds and extend their flowers above the foliage. Mostly warm colors are available; 'Jewel' includes some delicious pink and cherry shades. One of the best flowers for planted towers.

Nicotiana. Medium, mounded, heat-resistant, frost-tender, full-sun plant, like a taller petunia with tubular flowers. Comes in mostly soft colors. 'Domino' is reputedly fragrant, but the old-fashioned, much taller *N. affinis* is the sweetest of all.

Nolana napiformis. Small, trailing, heat-resistant, frost-tender, full-sun plants. Intense blue flowers like those of morning-glories, with white centers. The foliage is grayish green. Water sparingly.

Pansy (*Viola*). Small, mounded, cool-loving, very frost-hardy, sun-loving plants. The leading spring and fall flower for containers; intermittent winter bloom from Zone 6 south. Light shade will prolong summer bloom for a week or two. The distinction between pansies and violas is tenuous. Formerly, pansies had a "face" or "whisker" markings and violas had no markings. Hybridization has changed all that. Clear colors with no markings make the best edgings; pansies with faces or in mixed colors look better massed in groups. The 'Universal' series is quite popular; it has loads of medium-sized blossoms on short stems that stand up to rain.

Pentas. Medium to large, mounded, very heat- and humidity-resistant, full-sun plants, tender to frost. Once grown only along the Gulf Coast, pentas are proving successful for large containers north through Zone 6. Mostly soft colors are available.

Madagascar periwinkle (*Catharanthus roseus*). Small to medium, mounded to trailing, very heat- and humidity-resistant, full-sun, frost-tender plants. Very popular for enduring color under stressful conditions. Mostly soft colors are available, but 'Pink Panther' borders on red. The low-growing 'Magic Carpet' is best for hanging baskets. Unfortunately, this plant is often called vinca, but it should not be confused with the true vining vincas, *Vinca major* and *V. minor*.

Persian violet (*Exacum affine*). Small, mounded, cool-weather, frost-tender plants that need shade in warm climates. Use this as an edging plant in large containers. Fragrant violet-blue flowers.

Petunia. Medium, mounded to trailing, heat-resistant, sun-loving, somewhat frost-hardy plants. Very popular. The grandifloras have large, elaborate blossoms but are susceptible to botrytis (see Chapter 11). The many-flowered multifloras are disease-resistant and will endure more heat and drought. Modern breeding emphasis has been toward compact plants; if you want basket petunias, grow the older, more massive 'Cascade' types. The 'Daddy' series has contrasting, deeper-colored throats and veins. Double-flowered petunias are beautiful but not self-cleaning. Name a color except black, brown, and true blue and you'll find it in petunias.

Phlox (*Phlox drummondii*). Small, mounded, moderately heat- and frost-resistant, full-sun plants. An overlooked source of soft colors for edging containers. The plants are durable, free-blooming, and self-cleaning.

Dazzling verbenas, lantanas, and marigolds, with variegated vinca in a planter box.
PHOTO BY LINDA YANG

Poppy. Of the annual poppies, only the Iceland poppy is suited to container growing. A small, mounded, cool-weather, full-sun plant, it is too fragile for windy situations but is beloved for winter and early spring bloom in mild climates.

Blue salvia (*Salvia farinacea*). Medium to tall, erect, heat-resistant, full-sun perennial grown as an annual from Zone 6 north. Moderately frost-hardy. One of the best violet-blue or silver spike flowers for height accents. Constant color all summer.

Scarlet salvia (*Salvia splendens*). Small to medium, mounded to erect, heat-resistant, full-sun, frost-tender plants. Popular for bright red accents. 'Melba' is the shortest salvia, but the taller, more robust varieties remain in bloom longer. Purple, pink, and salmon cultivars are also available.

Snapdragon (dwarf). Small to medium, mounded, cool-loving, full-sun, moderately frost-resistant plants. Tall snaps are lovely, but need staking in containers. Grow the dwarfs, such as 'Floral Carpet' or 'Tahiti', as flowering ground covers in larger containers or in plunged pots. (To "plunge" pots, make planting holes and set the plants, pots and all, deep enough to hide the pots' rims. Plunging is used for short-term flowers because it minimizes transplant shock.) Many, many colors and bicolors are available in seed mixtures.

Strawflower (*Helichrysum*; dwarf). Medium, mounded, very heat-resistant, full-sun plants. Strawflowers suffer from being typed as an everlasting, but they will tolerate intense heat and dryness and continue to bloom. 'Bright Bikinis' has a startling array of pastel, vivid, and deep colors and glistening petals.

Sweet alyssum. Small, trailing, cool-weather, full-sun plants; hardy to light frosts. Available in white, purple, and lavender-pink. Precocious bloomer and prolific reseeder. The white form is the most fragrant.

Verbena. Small to medium, mounded to trailing, heat-resistant, full-sun, frost-tender plants. Garden verbena is more colorful than the perennial verbenas but is susceptible to leaf miners in some areas (see Chapter 11). 'Trinidad' is an outstanding vivid pink; 'Romance' is an excellent color mixture.

Wishbone flower (*Torenia*). Small to medium, mounded, very heat- and humidity-resistant, frost-tender plants, tolerant of light shade. An over-

A beautiful "mixed border" container planting of geraniums, lady's-mantle, lilies, and *Lychnis coronaria*.
PHOTO BY JERRY PAVIA

looked source of rain-or-shine color. Tough as a boot. Small but numerous flowers have fascinating color markings. The 'Clown' mixture contains blue, white, and pink with yellow or purple markings.

Zinnia (*Z. angustifolia* 'Classic'). Medium, mounded to trailing, very heat-, drought-, and humidity-resistant, full-sun, frost-tender plants. Yellow or orange flowers against narrow, willowy foliage. Rarely affected by mildew, the bane of other zinnias. Trails attractively. Worthy of greater popularity.

Creeping zinnia (*Sanvitalia procumbens*). Medium, trailing, very heat-, drought-, and humidity-resistant, sun-loving, frost-tender plant. Popular for hanging baskets or trailing over container rims. Not a true zinnia. Flowers are small, double, and numerous. A limited color range is available: yellow or orange with dark centers.

Perennials

Among the perennials are many extraordinarily beautiful plants that bloom or produce attractive foliage for prolonged periods but that are overlooked because most gardeners don't think about perennials when planting containers. Perennial plants usually cost more than annuals; many species are one-time, short-duration bloomers; and the best improved cultivars are generally available only from mail-order specialists. Yet a few perennial species are so outstanding, mature so quickly, and stand up so well to severe cold that no annual can match them as container plants.

The prime area for growing hardy perennials in the ground is Zone 4 through upper Zone 7, but alternate freezing and thawing makes it difficult to overwinter plants in containers without special protection. Consequently, northern container gardeners often transfer their perennials to beds in the ground in the fall, mulch them over the winter, and replant them in containers the following spring. Or they roll containers to an area where they can be set on the ground and mulched around and over, which keeps the containers from being destroyed and the roots from perishing in extreme cold. Sometimes all a gardener has to do is to plant in insulated containers and water during warm spells, when the planter mix thaws enough to accept water.

Color me purple—but lighten me with white and silver. Petunias, lobelias, ivy-leaved geraniums, pelargoniums, clematis, and dusty millers make a lively "foundation planting" for a modern house.

PHOTO BY DON NORMARK

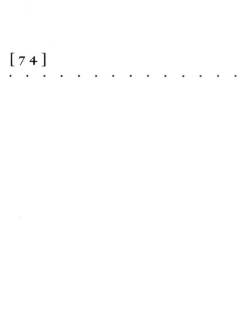

George Taloumis makes good use of the
steps to his porch. One year it may be
chrysanthemums in pots, another an
herb garden.

PHOTO BY GEORGE TALOUMIS

While the dogwoods brace for winter, a
large pot of 'Sky Magic' petunias and
'Dainty Marietta' marigolds go on
growing and glowing.

PHOTO BY ANN REILLY, PHOTO/NATS

Plumbago (*Ceratostigma plumbaginoides*). A handsome plant, low-growing and spreading, with green foliage that turns maroon in autumn. Blue flowers come in summer and autumn.

Potentilla. The best-known potentillas are spreading and yellow-flowered with five-fingered leaves. However, 'Gibson's Scarlet' makes a small, red-flowered bush that blooms all summer in the sun.

Primula. The common cowslip primrose (*Primula veris*) is one of the most popular perennials for winter bloom in warm climates and spring color elsewhere. Grow as a pot plant; plunge pots in groups if you want massed color. *P. obconica* and *P. malacoides* are favored for winter color in mild areas; both are so small that they should be grown in four- to six-inch pots.

Pulmonaria. A low-growing, compact, shade-tolerant, woodland foliage plant with silver-spotted green leaves. You can buy pink- or white-flowered varieties; the pink-flowered ones fade to blue with age.

Sedum spectabile. Medium-sized, mounded, heat-resistant, full-sun plants. Few annuals can match this hardy perennial for season-long show. Its fleshy silvery green leaves on multiple stems rising from the crown look neat all summer. Then, with the coming of fall, massive flat-tipped pink blossoms deepen in color with cold weather. 'Autumn Joy' is an autumn star, and attracts butterflies to add action to your garden.

***Snow-in-summer** (Cerastium tomentosum*). No other low-growing, fast-spreading perennial has such a desirable combination of numerous small, narrow, woolly white leaves and abundant white flowers. Extremely hardy and drought-resistant. The plants creep under and around taller plants and cascade over the edges of the container. They bloom in early summer but are attractive during the entire growing season.

Verbena. Several low-growing, base-branching cultivars have been selected from wild perennial verbenas. All are heat- and humidity-resistant, are troubled little by leaf miners, and make durable, long-blooming plants for hanging baskets and tubs. Cultivars of the rose verbena (*V. canadensis*) are available in fragrant rose, white, lavender, and purple. The lilac Dakota vervain (*V. bipinnatifida*) has finely cut foliage. The very hardy moss vervain (*V. tenuisecta*) is available in blue, violet, lilac, and white cultivars. You may have difficulty distinguishing one species from another without looking closely at the leaves.

Vinca (*V. minor* and *V. major*; periwinkle or vine myrtle). This is the true vinca, not the Madagascar periwinkle, *Catharanthus roseus*, which is sometimes improperly called vinca. These heat- and humidity-resistant evergreen trailers are covered with violet-blue flowers in the spring. Often used in hanging baskets and as a ground cover in containers planted with spring bulbs. Happy in full sun but will tolerate light shade, especially the large-leaved *V. major* with variegated foliage.

Perennials seem to have minds of their own. Young plants will sometimes not bloom until the year following planting, and some are late to emerge from the ground; be sure to stick a label by the plant so you won't forget and try to plant something on top of its root in spring.

Bulbs

Bulbous plants, which grow quickly from food reserves stored in their fleshy bulbs, corms, tubers, or rhizomes, combine naturally with annuals or perennials that bloom at the same time. Low-growing flowers fill in around the rather sparse, erect, bulbous plants like little children clinging to their mother's skirt.

One of the hidden assets of plants that grow from bulbs is their ability to entertain and amaze you by the transformations in their development. They are a delight to watch as they push up spears, buds, and leaves. Try growing bulbs by themselves in containers the first season to get the hang of planting and a feel for when you can expect them to bloom. Then, the following year, you will be able to add some annuals or perennials with confidence. An underplanting of dainty johnny-jump-ups among the tulips does add a finishing touch.

SPRING-BLOOMING BULBS

For spring bloom, plant narcissus and other hardy spring bulbs in rather shallow containers of one- to three-gallon capacity in fall or winter. Moisten the soil and set the containers in a protected place so that they remain cool and grow roots but do not freeze clear through during the winter. Water once a month, then set them outdoors when the weather

Dozens of fragrant hyacinths in a concrete bowl tie the corner of
the deck to the landscape beyond.

Color your corners with a dozen bulbs of
regal lilies in a shallow seven-gallon
terra-cotta container.

PHOTO BY THOMAS E. ELTZROTH

starts to warm up. Often you can buy preplanted pots of bulbs primed for early bloom by storage in a cool area after planting. If you plant your own bulbs, ask your dealer whether they have been precooled; this is most important where winters are mild.

Successions of **narcissi** chosen for early, second early, and midspring bloom work best in containers. For starters, plant paper-white narcissi in midwinter and force growth indoors for early spring color and fragrance; set the containers outside on mild days. The fragrant pheasant-eye or poet's narcissi started at the same time will come into bloom next, and last of all the large-flowered trumpet narcissi.

Any of the narcissi except the tiny species, such as hoop-petticoat daffodils, look great in basin-shaped three-gallon containers. The hoop-petticoats are dear little things but are so small they can muster the strength only to whisper that spring is here. Plant the tiny species close together in six-inch bulb-pan pots; group three to five pots in a shallow container, fill in around them with gravel, and set them on a high pedestal so you can admire the flowers close up.

Fragrant **hyacinths** make even better container plants than narcissi because of their greater range of colors and their fragrance. Plant hyacinth bulbs three to four inches apart, because the leaves are more wide-spreading than those of daffodils and don't look good when plants are crowded together. Hyacinths come into bloom right after the paper-whites.

Tulips are the premier spring container plants. Like narcissi and hyacinths, they will bloom earlier and more strongly if planted in late fall and wintered over in a cool, dark place where root growth can begin. Alternatively, if your dealer can assure that the bulbs have been precooled, you can plant them in midwinter. Top growth won't commence until you move the container to a sunny, warm spot. You have your choice of the unusual species types or the conventional early, cottage, Darwin, lily-flowered, or parrot tulips.

An underplanting of cool-loving annuals can disguise the yellowing foliage of tulips as they mature. You do not need to space the tulips widely; after the bulbs have emerged and you have moved the container outdoors, set seedlings of annuals among them, and they will knit into a solid underplanting and bloom with and after the tulips. Violas, pansies, stocks, calendulas, perennial white candytuft, sweet alyssum, English daisies, forget-me-nots, and primulas of various species are popular for interplanting. Some of these are technically perennials but are handled as annuals. You have a greater choice of companion plants than with narcissi and hyacinths, because tulips bloom later.

Consider the exotic **fritillaries** if you want a change from tulips in containers. The crown imperial and the checker lily shoot up rather tall stems; space the bulbs six to eight inches apart in five- to seven-gallon tubs. The odor of fritillaries is hardly noticeable outdoors, but don't plan on decorating a room with them!

The so-called small bulbs — **snowdrops, snowflakes, crocuses, grape hyacinths, stars-of-Bethlehem, chionodoxas,** and **scillas** — display better when massed, in containers as well as in garden beds. A scattering of bulbs among annual flowers is too insubstantial to create color impact in containers. Plant them as you would the tiny narcissi.

Some container gardeners sacrifice spring bulbs after they have bloomed. (Indeed, there is no point in saving tulips in Zone 7 and south, because one season of bloom is all you can expect.) If you want to save your bulbs, you generally have the best chance if you plant all of one kind in one container, so you can set the pot aside after the blooms are spent. After the foliage has turned brown and the growth cycle has been completed, dump the mature bulbs and sun-dry them for winter storage. However, if you need the containers for summer plantings, transplant the bulbs to a corner of the garden and harvest them when the tops have dried completely. Don't expect all the bulbs you save after a season in containers to bloom the next year; they may need a year of recuperation in the garden to rebuild food reserves. To be certain of a showy display, you may want to plant the used bulbs in the garden and buy new ones for your containers.

In addition to the hardy spring bulbs, a few tender varieties look stunning in containers. **Amaryllis,** commonly thought of as a spring-blooming houseplant, makes an excellent specimen plant for windowboxes and freestanding containers. The large bulbs can be forced in the usual six-inch pots in which they are sold and plunged into the soil of containers after danger of frost. Forcing should not commence until about thirty days prior to the spring frost-free date. Knock the bulbs out of their pots after they have bloomed and set them in the garden to grow on until fall. At that time, you can take them up, dry them out, and save them for potting up the following spring.

Anemones and **ranunculuses** are fairly similar flowers that are often seen in containers in the West and Northwest, where they bloom in the spring from fall plantings. You couldn't ask for much brighter flowers to come in at tulip time. They will do pretty well across the northern states from spring planting, but they resent hot, humid days. You can grow anemones and ranunculuses from their wispy little tubers, or, in the West and Northwest, you can buy potted plants.

Freesias are in the same class of frost-tender, cool-loving bulbous plants; they like to flower during the short days of winter and early spring and are best adapted where winters are mild. Elsewhere, gardeners can bloom them in a cool greenhouse, then bring them into the house where their vivid colors and fragrance can be enjoyed. A hanging basket of fragrant freesias is a real show-stopper.

Calla lilies, technically species of *Zantedeschia*, are winter- and spring-blooming rhizomatous plants that like a dry, almost dormant resting period during the summer. Don't confuse them with cannas, which flourish during the summer. Callas are of little value for containers north of Zone 7 because they are only half-hardy. Where they are adapted, grow them in light shade and set the containers aside after bloom. Let the rhizomes dry out for a month or two, then repot them in new planter mix in the fall. Commercial growers are beginning to force dwarf zantedeschias in pots for spring sale; these can be set outdoors for color spots if you protect them from frost.

Plant all the summer bulbs except lilies late enough in the spring to escape frost damage. Summer bulbs usually bloom longer than any of the spring species. If you wish to save the bulbs, set the container aside and grow the plants to maturity in order to rebuild the food reserves.

Many summer bulbs grow so tall that they require staking, which is not easy to accomplish with container plants. Tall dahlias, tall lilies, standard gladioli, eremurus or foxtail lilies, and standard tall agapanthus or lilies-of-

SUMMER-
BLOOMING
BULBS

□ □ □

the-Nile are best left for the garden or planted in containers large enough to balance their height. Look for bulbs, tubers, corms, or rhizomes of dwarf varieties that require no staking. The miniature varieties of gladioli grow only twelve to sixteen inches tall, and their bulbs are easy to dry and store for replanting in the spring.

The leading summer bulbs for containers are the garden **lilies**, especially the short-top Asiatics. Certain of the candelabra martagons with pendent blossoms are short enough to make good container plants. If you want fragrance, you will need to choose the taller trumpet lilies. Insert bamboo stakes around the edge of the container, all the way to the bottom, and run wires around them to prevent the plants from blowing over or breaking.

Unlike other summer bulbs, lilies are hardy and can be potted up in fall, along with tulips and daffodils, and given moderate protection. The earlier you plant lily bulbs, the earlier they will bloom — within limits, of course. If you plant them in the fall, they will begin to bloom in early summer, depending on the species. If you plant them in the spring, they will begin to bloom in midsummer. Most species like fairly acid soil and abundant moisture; all benefit from light shade in the afternoon.

Lily bulbs are too valuable to risk in containers outdoors over winter without protection. You could probably get by safely in Zone 7 and south, but further north you run the risk of injuring the bulbs with the combination of cold and dryness in containers. Dump the containers in the fall, after the bulbs have rebuilt their food reserves, and remove any small bulblets for growing on in a separate pot. Wash and scald the container and replant the mother bulbs in fresh planter mix. Moisten the mix and set the container indoors in a cool area. You can also store the bulbs separately and pot them up in spring; just don't let them dry out too much.

The **dwarf dahlias** run lilies a close second as summer-blooming container plants and can be planted in the spring. The tubers sprout and grow quickly, but don't set the container outside until danger of frost is past. Dwarf dahlias top off at twelve to twenty-four inches and are moderately heat-resistant. Where summers are cool, they will bloom from midsummer through fall. Some cultivars have purplish bronze foliage, which is handsome at all stages of growth. Dahlias will winter over in containers in Zone 7 and south, but the tubers can rot during wet years. Dump the containers

This garden is located on an eastern slope in San Luis Obispo, California. The residents are elderly people who do not like working and digging on the slope. Morning sunlight opens up the yellow oxalis, which makes a dramatic area against the tubs of emperor tulips.

PHOTO BY KRISTI JONES

in the fall, prune off the top growth a few inches above the tubers, and store them in a cool, dry, dark area. In the spring, separate them carefully, leaving an "eye" on each tuber, and replant in fresh planter mix.

The new dwarf varieties of heat-resistant **cannas** make fine summer-blooming container plants. The plants are short, with wide, tropical-looking leaves, and need ten- to fifteen-gallon containers. Cannas stay in bloom for up to forty-five days, and the foliage is attractive at other times. Most gardeners are not aware that cannas will grow as aquatic plants. Set containers in pools so their bottoms are two or three inches below the water line, and the plants will perform beautifully. Take up and store the rhizomes in the fall.

Consider **caladiums** in containers to add foliage color to lightly or moderately shaded areas. They grow from corms, which look like bulbs but have no scales. When fall comes, you can save the corms for replanting, but it isn't easy, as they tend to dry out or rot. Your biggest decision in choosing cultivars of caladiums is which color will look best in your garden. The silver and green variegations are perhaps the most soothing and useful; the reds, maroons, and pinks require care in siting. Shaded windowboxes planted thickly with caladiums can brighten drab walls. Few ornamentals are more heat-resistant, but you must water frequently to keep the large, thin leaves from wilting.

If you want a summer-blooming bulb that will make people say, "Wow! Would you look at that!" try **giant allium**. When well grown, the round head of tightly clustered purple flowers can reach five inches or more in diameter. Giant alliums grow quite tall but are so strong they don't need staking. Because of the size of the plant, start with a five- to seven-gallon container, preferably a squat tub that won't tip over.

A summer bulb that deserves greater attention is *Lycoris*. The several species have colorful common names, such as naked ladies, naked lilies, surprise lilies, rain lilies, resurrection lilies, and so on; these are derived from the plant's habit of shooting up a leafless stem topped by an airy cluster of flowers. Bulbs of *Lycoris* in containers won't survive winters north of Zone 7 or 8, and are planted in the spring. Put the container outside when all danger of frost is past. The plants' performance improves with age. Leave the bulbs in the same container until the blooms begin running down in size, then repot. *Lycoris* goes through dormant periods when no top growth shows; go easy on watering during these times. Combine *Lycoris* with low-growing summer annuals, so it can shoot up through them and bloom above the flowering underplanting.

Agapanthus, or lily-of-the-Nile, is often used as a container plant in California but can be grown elsewhere if you take the plant indoors during the winter and let it dry partially. Technically, the grasslike evergreen plant is not bulbous but has a thick rootstock. The basal rosette of leaves is rather large, so you should plant only one per three- to five-gallon container. The dwarf white and blue cultivars are in scale with these rather small pots.

Growing bulbs, tubers, corms, or rhizomes in containers is difficult for frugal gardeners because it sometimes means discarding the plants after they have bloomed. However, gardeners who make the best use of their containers and the space available to them routinely weed out ornamentals when they are over the hill, and have replacements ready to plug in. I think they see landscapes as dynamic paintings, where fresh accents of color can be splashed as spent plants fade. They regard plants as a means to an end, rather than an end in themselves. Whatever their motives and gratifications, they are growing in numbers, and their influence is enhancing the art of maintaining color in containers during every month of the growing season.

. . . .

F or once, I'm going to be a "lumper" rather than a "splitter" and throw all plants without backbone into this section. If they can't stand erect, and if they throw out limber, pliant growth that clings, clambers, hangs, or creeps, you'll find them listed here, whether they are annual flowering vines, hardy perennial vines, or tropical flowering or foliage vines.

Vines in containers fill specialized niches in landscapes. They can be trained up posts or arbors to beautify them, trained up strings or mesh to make living screens, or pegged to walls to break up monotonous lines. Annuals or fast-growing perennials will vine to cover mesh stretched over an outdoor living area to cast shade. Allowed to trail, vines make graceful additions to hanging baskets and windowboxes. As a general rule, though,

Vines

Opposite: Old World charm
at Butchart Gardens near Victoria, on
Vancouver Island, B.C. The wall of the
house is covered with ivy and decked
with three levels of plants in
windowboxes, hanging baskets, and
pots on the patio.

PHOTO BY JOANNE PAVIA

Right: A close-up of one section of the
wall at Butchart Gardens shows a
hanging basket over two windowboxes,
with potted geraniums at ground level.

PHOTO BY JERRY PAVIA

Dusk-to-dawn color for night owls. The
flowers of the fragrant moonflower vine
open in the evening. In cloudy weather
and on cool fall days, the flowers stay
open well into the next day.

PHOTO BY GEORGE TALOUMIS

the twining vines don't make good hanging-basket subjects, because of the stubborn geotropism that commands them to climb.

A few vines of modest size, such as the large-flowered clematis cultivars, ivy, creeping fig, and grape ivy, can be grown in three- to five-gallon containers, but most require the ten-gallon size or larger. Some of the tropical vines are simply too large and fast-growing to remain for more than a season or two in a container, even a fifty-gallon box. In Zones 4 and 5, you can use smaller containers than I have recommended here, because warmth-loving vines grow more slowly where nights are cool, and never attain the size they do further south or west.

The annual flowering vines, which may be perennial in warm climates, include many excellent and fast-growing species. Some, such as morning-glory, open just before dawn and close by midmorning, except on gloomy days. Others, such as moon vine, open just after dusk and close at dawn. Those with longer-lasting flowers remain open but close slightly during the brightest part of the day. Most of the annual flowering vines are twiners.

You can grow some of the frost-vulnerable species as annuals in Zones 6, 7, and 8 and as perennials in protected areas of Zones 9 and 10. However, some of the tropicals require so much heat to grow to flowering size that they won't perform well in the North or coastal Northwest. Some of the species usually grown in small containers as houseplants can be set outside during summer months if you gradually harden them off to the wind and if you grow them in light shade.

Aristolochia. Perennial. The hardy eastern native, *A. durior*, and the western wild vine, *A. californica*, are both commonly known as Dutchman's pipe. These are old-fashioned vines for screening porches and are not much in favor today. The large kidney- or heart-shaped leaves overlap like shingles and hide the curious greenish flowers, shaped like a meerschaum pipe. The vines are rampant and need training. Vines, flowers, and seeds are poisonous.

Bougainvillea. Woody tender perennial. Widely planted throughout Zones 9 and 10, the vivid bougainvillea is moving north through sales of plants in full bloom in three- to five-gallon pots or hanging baskets. Plants need to be shifted up each year to a larger container. Only in the Deep

South and warm West does bougainvillea climb as strongly as wisteria; elsewhere, it looks more like a limber shrub. The standard southern or western form is a woody vine that is usually trained up a post to support its considerable weight. Vines can withstand light frosts but prefer to be brought into a sunny, cool room for the winter.

Campsis. Hardy woody vine. Formerly known as *Bignonia*, this genus includes the invasive woody trumpet creepers, native to the eastern United States. The Chinese trumpet creeper (*C. grandiflora*) is not as aggressive and has larger, tubular scarlet flowers. Grow it in five- to ten-gallon containers and train the fast-growing shoots up strong strings or a trellis.

Cissus. Grape ivy (*C. rhombifolia*), kangaroo vine (*C. antartica*), and rex-begonia vine (*C. discolor*) are a few of the ornamental tender perennial vines in this genus, grown mostly for their attractive foliage. They are tough and adaptable, climb by tendrils, and prefer moderately shaded locations. Grow them in large hanging baskets or to trail down over the edges of window-boxes in shaded areas.

Clematis. Many hardy, deciduous varieties of garden clematis will do well in containers if the tops are in the sun and the containers are shaded in the afternoon. Clematis vines don't twine; they display best when trained or allowed to grow up netting or a trellis. Grow hardy clematis in three- to five-gallon containers. Trim the plants back somewhat and move the containers into a basement for the winter, or bank them up with soil to lessen the effect of cold. The tender evergreen species such as *C. armandii* are best grown in larger containers (ten to fifteen gallons) in Zones 7, 8, and 9, where they will produce their fragrant white blooms in early spring.

Clerodendrum. Tender perennial. The species *C. thomsoniae*, or bleeding-heart vine, is the best known. A strong, frost-tender climber, it is popular for hanging baskets because it will climb the supports if trained. The clusters of flowers are so large that they don't show to best advantage on vines allowed to trail. The white, red-centered flowers are among the most handsome on any species. Grow in three- to five-gallon baskets in filtered or dappled sunlight; protect from full afternoon sun.

Cobaea. Tender annual. The species *C. scandens*, cup-and-saucer vine, grows quite large where summers are long and rather cool. If grown on the eastern or northern side of a house, shaded from the afternoon sun, it can

A two-gallon pot is all this Canary Island ivy needs to decorate an entire wall.
PHOTO BY JOHN NEUBAUER

Sweet peas for late spring color and
aroma. When the hot weather does them
in, you can replace the whole container,
trellis and all, with a summer-flowering
vine like the black-eyed-Susan vine on
page 100.

thrive further south. The large, curious, bell-shaped flowers are purple, lavender, or white; they are surrounded by a large green calyx shaped like a saucer. Grow in ten- to fifteen-gallon tubs and train the heavy vines up strong supports.

Cryptostegia. Tender tropical. Also known as purple allamanda or rubber vine, this milkweed family member grows best where summers are extremely long and warm (Zones 9 and 10). The species *C. grandiflora* has purple flowers two to three inches in diameter, with flaring petals over short tubes. Plant this rapid grower in ten- to fifteen-gallon tubs and run the vines up wires.

Dioscorea. This is a genus of the frost-tender tropical yam group, which includes the beautifully variegated foliage vine *D. discolor*, the strange elephant's foot or hottentot-bread (*D. elephantipes*), and the air potato (*D. bulbifera*), with aerial, angled tubers. All are better suited to containers in Zone 8 and south, where the tubers can increase in size over the years. Grow in fifteen- to thirty-gallon containers and provide strong, tall supports for the rampant vines.

Dolichos. Frost-tender annuals. The species *D. lablab*, or hyacinth bean, is a beautiful, heat-resistant annual vine easily grown from seeds. The vines are tinged with purple, and the dark purple pods, which are shaped like limas, are edible when young but become fibrous when full-size. The Australian pea vine (*D. lignosus*) is seldom seen outside of the cooler areas of California, where its tender perennial vines produce hundreds of curious rose-purple flowers and curled seedpods. Both grow rapidly by twining, and need containers of at least ten-gallon capacity. Easy to grow.

Eccremocarpus. Tender perennial, difficult to grow. This is a spectacular clinging vine that can be grown from early-started seeds to bloom the first year. Also called Chilean glory flower, *E. scaber* has been improved to include pink, orange, yellow, and red shades. Flowers are borne in loose heads; leaves are finely cut. Slow to bloom, and only moderately heat-resistant. Grow in five- to ten-gallon baskets or buckets.

Ficus. Tropical. The creeping fig (*F. pumila*) is an easy-to-grow, small-leaved, shade-loving, frost-tender vine which can be run up "poles" made of chicken wire stuffed with long-fiber sphagnum moss. The numerous branches cling by holdfasts. Rather slow-growing where seasons are short;

hardy in Zones 8 through 10, marginally hardy in Zone 7. Much used for covering topiary armatures or forms stuffed with sphagnum moss.

Hedera. This is the ivy genus; the range of shapes, sizes, and colors of leaves is sufficient to meet anyone's ideal of a vine for foliage. The highly ornamental cultivars will usually winter over in southern Zone 6; plant the more rugged perennials farther north. English ivy (*H. helix*) includes many varieties with variegated and deeply cut foliage. Typically, ivy is used as a trailing vine in hanging baskets or to soften the edges of windowboxes or planter boxes. The fancy varieties grow rather slowly and can be reproduced from cuttings when the mother plants become too large for your containers.

Humulus. Perennial, usually grown as an annual. The common hop vine (*H. lupulus*), grown as a bitter flavoring for beer, is an old-fashioned, rambling, rampant vine with greenish flowers. The exotic *H. japonicus* has foliage streaked with white. Will live over except where winters are quite severe. Needs tubs or boxes of fifteen- to twenty-gallon size.

Ipomoea. Tropical perennial, grown as an annual. This large genus includes the twining morning-glory vines; the night-blooming, fragrant white moon vine (*I. alba*); the small-flowered, ferny-leaved cypress vine (*I. quamoclit*); the larger-flowered cardinal climber (*I. × multifida*); and the native North American red star vine (*I. coccinea*). All are easily grown from seeds, flower within a few weeks, and are relatively pest-free. Moon vine and morning-glory (*I. tricolor*) have the heaviest vines; cypress vine, the most fernlike. Grow in ten- to fifteen-gallon tubs or boxes in full sun; if you try to grow them in hanging baskets, the tendrils will form unsightly tangles by trying to climb up descending vines.

Jasminum. The true jasmines are frost-tender, perennial woody vines and, although best adapted to Zones 8 and 9, are often grown farther north, where gardeners move the containers indoors during cold weather. *J. officinale*, the common white jasmine, has highly fragrant flowers. *J. polyanthum* blooms when quite small, with fragrant white flowers tinged with pink. First blooms appear in early spring. Grow in five- to ten-gallon containers or large hanging baskets.

Lapageria. Frost-tender perennial. The extraordinarily beautiful national flower of Chile is easily grown only where summers are cool and winters are mild — specifically, in coastal southern and central California. This is a

An arbor post festooned with hanging pots of asparagus fern, petunias, and lantana. Ivy twines from a pot on the deck.
PHOTO BY GARY MOTTAU

twining vine with large pendent flowers shaped like hoop skirts. Pink, lavender, and carmine in *L. rosea* and white in the 'Alba' variety, lapageria can be grown in five- to ten-gallon containers.

Mandevilla. A large genus of frost-tender, mostly South American vines. One cultivar, 'Alice du Pont', is growing in importance for large hanging baskets. A tender perennial, it will regrow and flower in Zone 6 and south if cut back and protected from freezing. In the north, mandevilla needs to be forced into flower in a greenhouse or under fluorescent lights before being moved outdoors. The pink flowers are quite large, up to four inches across, and the heart-shaped foliage is attractive. Resists heat and humidity; begins flowering while plants are small.

Mina. The species *M. lobata* (Spanish flag) is much like the *Ipomoea* species called cypress vine or hearts-and-honey vine, except that the lobed leaves are heart-shaped where they join the petiole. The many small red flowers fade to yellow with age. Grows quickly from seeds; treat as an annual where summers are short. Grow in five- to ten-gallon containers and train up strings; not rampant.

Mucuna. Frost-tender tropical, hardy in Zone 9. The genus includes velvet bean (*M. deeringiana*), the familiar forage crop of the South, and the showy tropical climber *M. bennettii*, with sprays of orange-red blossoms shaped like claws. In Victorian days velvet bean was used to shade porches, but it is rather ordinary-looking beside the more colorful *M. bennettii*. Adapted only where summers are long and warm. Grow from seeds in fifteen- to twenty-gallon containers.

Passiflora. The passionflower genus, rich in religious significance, includes not only the hardy native maypop of the South but also many exotic tropical vines of great beauty. The tender hybrid *P. × alatocaerulea*, with white blossoms marked with purple and pink, is the most popular. Hardy to Zone 7, it can be cut back and overwintered indoors in the North. Often seen in warmer climates is the tender red passionflower (*P. coccinea*) and the edible purple granadilla or passion fruit (*P. edulis*). The vines of passionflowers are heavy and need support; grow in ten- to fifteen-gallon containers. When plants become potbound, cut the bottoms out of the containers and plunge them in thirty- to fifty-gallon tubs or half barrels to avoid damaging the root systems.

A trellis attached to the back of a planter box supports a climbing black-eyed-Susan vine, *Thunbergia alata,* which will flower all summer.

PHOTO BY THOMAS E. ELTZROTH

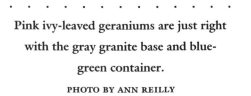

. . . .
Pink ivy-leaved geraniums are just right
with the gray granite base and blue-
green container.

PHOTO BY ANN REILLY

Philodendron and *Scindapsus*. Tropicals, grown outdoors in Zones 9 and 10 and in Zone 8 by covering against frosts. Such large-leaved tropicals like moderate shade and frequent spraying or sprinkling to keep humidity high. Many of the philodendrons are upright, large-leaved plants that make handsome specimens in seven- to ten-gallon tubs. However, the common heart-leaf philodendron (*P. scandens*) can be trained up posts of bark or moss or allowed to trail, as can the larger-leaved panda plant (*P. bipennifolium*) and the colorful red-leaf or blushing philodendron (*P. erubescens*). Grow them in three- to five-gallon containers. A similar species, once called pothos, *Scindapsus pictus* 'Argyraeus', is a fleshy-stemmed climber with green leaves marked with silvery spots. Northerners view these as houseplants, not realizing how large and spectacular they can grow outdoors in the Deep South and warm West.

Piper. This genus includes the tropical vine that produces peppers for spice, but the species most commonly grown in containers is *P. crocatum*, with colorful variegated leaves and crimson undersides. The slender, frost-tender vines need high humidity, support, and afternoon shade. Grow in five- to ten-gallon containers. Difficult.

Rhodochiton. One tender perennial species, *R. atrosanguineum*, will flower the first year from early-started seeds. It is adapted to cool-summer areas such as coastal southern California but can be forced into bloom early indoors in Zones 4 and 5 and set outside after danger of frost. The vine bears pink, umbrella-like flowers with extended purple-black tubular centers and has heart-shaped leaves. Vines need support. This is the sort of plant that wins at flower shows because of its curious flowers. Grow in one- to three-gallon pots and train up strings.

Rhoicissus. The easy-to-grow evergreen grapevine (*R. capensis*) is grown for foliage. A common houseplant, hardy in Zone 8 and south, the vine needs afternoon shade and rich soil to grow rapidly in outdoor containers. It can be trained up or allowed to trail down the sides of windowboxes or hanging baskets.

Stephanotis. The tender woody vine known as floradora or waxflower (*S. floribunda*) has extremely fragrant, waxy white flowers, valued for weddings. It is quite frost-tender but heat-resistant if the containers, like those of clematis, are given some shade. If you move it to protection for the winter, cut back on watering several days before the move to lessen the shock of dry air. Stephanotis can be finicky about blooming and is vulnerable to pests. Grow in three- to five-gallon pots.

Thunbergia. Annual. This genus includes the familiar short-vined, quick-flowering black-eyed-Susan vine (*T. alata*), with white, yellow, or orange blossoms, some with black centers. Often grown in hanging baskets or windowboxes. Individual plants don't need large containers; the three-gallon size is sufficient. *T. alata* has yellowish green clambering vines, which can be tied up or allowed to trail. The woody tropical clock vine (*T. grandiflora*) has much more vigorous vines and large blue or white flowers. Grow it in ten- to fifteen-gallon containers.

Tropaeolum. Tender perennial grown as an annual. Two common species of the nasturtium genus grow stems long enough to be called vines. The canary-bird vine (*T. peregrinum*) needs to be trained up a trellis, where in cool-summer areas it will produce a good crop of curiously birdlike yellow blossoms against sparse five-lobed leaves. Grow in hanging baskets eighteen inches in diameter or larger. The so-called climbing nasturtium (*T. majus*) is really an old-fashioned variety with open, spreading growth and long runners. It has naturalized in shaded glens in parts of California. Grow in two- to three-gallon pots or baskets. Both species burn out in hot weather and are susceptible to aphid damage. Nasturtium and canary-vine flowers are esteemed by chefs for their nippy flavor.

Cacti, Succulents, and Yuccas

Cacti, succulents, and yuccas look and perform best when planted with each other in containers, not mixed with herbaceous or woody plants. Desert cacti and succulents are, in the main, native to arid countries. Where they grow wild in humid regions, they are restricted to sun-baked banks or deep sandy soils. As container plants, they need full sun except in the hottest desert areas, where a bit of afternoon shade reduces stress. Jungle cacti, in contrast, grow wild in the crotches of trees or in organic matter trapped on shady, rocky slopes. In containers, they need shade from direct sun at midday and through the hottest part of the afternoon.

The prime climatic region for growing cacti and succulents in containers

is the low-elevation country of Arizona, New Mexico, and west Texas. Winters there are so dry that few plants die from rotting. Southern California is almost as well suited, but you may have to roll your plants under an overhang during the torrential rains that sometimes come during the winter. Cacti and succulents are popular in south Texas and south Florida, but the frost-tender types have to be rolled into garages during cold spells. (I say "rolled" because large cacti are too prickly to pick up, and large succulents are too brittle.)

Elsewhere in the country, cacti and succulents must be treated as houseplants during the winter. You may be tempted to discard them in the fall, but the plants increase so much in value every year that they are well worth keeping. After a few seasons, inexpensive plants that started out in three-inch pots grow into specimens or dish gardens of considerable value.

Large plants of choice cacti and succulents are expensive because they grow so slowly. If you buy large native species of cacti, succulents, or yuccas, please inquire about their origin and accept only nursery-grown plants. Despite strict laws protecting endangered species, unscrupulous people still dig them from the wild.

I don't recommend that families with children plant spiny cacti, or yuccas or agaves with dagger-pointed leaves. Neither do I recommend large, spiny, or sharp-pointed plants for older gardeners, because they can be heavy and have to be moved with care. Yet that eliminates only a few varieties; you still have many desirable species to choose from.

All of these plants require a fast-draining soil mix to prevent root rot. Make it by adding one part of coarse, screened sand or perlite to two parts of standard planter mix. You may have to shift fast-growing specimens into the next largest pot size each spring, and slower-growing species every two years. When plants grow so large that their containers are difficult to move, knock out the plant, scrape some of the old roots off the the root ball, and set the plant back in the same pot with a top-dressing of new planter mix.

Cacti and succulents are customarily grown in terra-cotta or concrete pots, not only because they look good against earth colors but because these porous pots evaporate more water than plastic ones do. Large, rather shallow basins are quite popular. Their surface area is greater in proportion to their capacity than that of cylindrical pots, and they stay drier.

Terra-cotta containers take on a wonderful patina with age. In this nicely rounded one, gray succulents are topped by plants of Moses-in-the-cradle.
PHOTO BY LINDA YANG

Grow cacti and succulents indoors in winter, in a cool room or on an unheated sunporch. A temperature of 50-55°F is ideal. They will tolerate greater extremes; witness the huge plants growing happily outdoors in mild areas where winter temperatures often hover around 40°F. They will also survive in a room that is warmer than 55°. Water desert species monthly during their winter resting period, weekly during their active growth period, and twice weekly in extremely dry weather. Jungle cacti require more frequent watering but like rather dry soil during the cool winter months. Cacti and succulents are not heavy feeders but respond to liquid feeding every two to four weeks after flowering is completed. Feed them only when they are putting on new growth.

When you have to move, separate, or repot cacti, handle the spiny varieties with great care. Wrap them in canvas or a heavy cloth that won't be impaled on the spines, and wear heavy gloves.

Many species and cultivars of cacti and succulents are so small that they are best suited to growing as houseplants in small pots. All of them start out small, of course, but it is difficult to know their ultimate potential size. Some, such as the agaves called century plants, can grow into huge specimens, yet some of the mature sedums can be contained in a teacup.

Some large species, such as the barrel cacti, agaves, and crassulas, display best as single specimens in containers selected to show off the color and shape of the individual plant. But most cacti and succulents are planted as dish gardens in which smaller, lower-growing specimens cluster around taller, more dominant kinds, such as the yuccas or *Cereus peruvianus*. Dish gardens are difficult to shift to larger pots intact. When your garden is ready for more growing space or you want to separate clustered plants, use the opportunity to arrange the components into a new dish landscape.

The best assortments of desert cacti and succulents are offered by nurseries and specialists in desert regions, but the choices elsewhere are increasing every year as more people discover the charm of these specialized plants.

I haven't attempted to single out noteworthy cultivars for your attention but have listed the major genera that have proved best for container growing. Remember, in much of the country, cacti and succulents are sold as houseplants, while quite small. You will have to ask your nursery or refer to a book for information on how a particular plant will look a few years hence.

This weathered wood planter graces an old wooden gate at the entrance to the gardens at The Herbfarm in Fall City, Washington. The plants are easy-to-care-for succulents.

PHOTO BY DON NORMARK

Cacti in nests of green and red alternanthera in a
cast-concrete bowl.

PHOTO BY GEORGE TALOUMIS

An inexpensive but useful publication, especially for the East, is the Brooklyn Botanic Garden's *Handbook on Succulent Plants*.

CACTI

□ □ □

Cereus. Some of the most dramatic, tall, columnar cacti are in this genus. *C. peruvianus* is the best known. The tall columns have five to eight vertical ribs, clusters of marginal spines, and large, fragrant white flowers. The oddly attractive, contorted cultivar 'Monstrosus' is branched, knobby, and twisted.

Echinocactus. Several barrel cacti are in this species. Some varieties are greenish gold; others are more green. The numerous spiny ribs become deeply indented with age. The species *E. horizonthalonius*, often sold as a houseplant, is rather small and blooms at an earlier age than others.

Epiphyllum. This is the famous night-blooming cereus or orchid cactus. A jungle genus, its members are more tolerant of water than desert cacti and need shade from afternoon sun. The long, notched, flattened stems bear enormous, fragrant nocturnal flowers in pink, red, or white. Epiphyllums are customarily grown alone in pots hung high on walls or in hanging baskets, and are easy to grow.

Ferocactus. The barrel-shaped fishhook cactus is aptly named, as the fierce spines are hooked in some varieties. *F. acanthodes* is a large green plant; *F. latispinus* is smaller and gray-green.

Heliocereus. The sun cactus (*H. speciosus*) makes a beautiful hanging-basket plant. The long, slim, four-lobed stems arch and trail to three feet. One of the jungle cacti, it needs shade from midday and afternoon sun.

Rhipsalidopsis and ***Schlumbergera.*** The familiar Christmas cactus, the Easter cactus, and the lesser-known Thanksgiving cactus are in this group. Grow these jungle species in standard potting soils rather than the dry, fast-draining mixes preferred by desert cacti. Old plants arch gracefully and display well in hanging baskets or containers on high pedestals. Foliage color gives a pretty good index of when these plants need feeding; normally, the foliage is deep green.

Many small species of desert cacti offer clustering plants to place around the bases of larger species. *Astrophytum*, *Echinopsis* (sea-urchin cactus), *Gymnocalycium* (chin cactus), *Lobivia* (cob cactus), *Mammillaria*, *Notocactus*, and *Rebutia* (crown cactus) are among the better types.

SUCCULENTS

□ □ □

Aeonium. These somewhat resemble the crassulas, or jade plants. All have rosettes of fleshy purplish or silvery green leaves. Some species have long, lax, fleshy stems with rosettes on the ends; others are stemless and mound-like.

Agave. Agaves have rosettes of fleshy, sword-shaped leaves, some green or bluish, some edged with creamy yellow or pure white. I prefer the smaller ones, such as *A. victoriae-reginae*, which grows to a maximum height of about one foot and has attractive raised white spots on the leaves.

Aloe. These somewhat resemble the agaves but generally have thinner leaves, spiny or hooked in some species. Look for the small species *A. variegata*, which includes the variety called partridge-breast. It is gray-green, with contrasting white barring. The medicinal aloe, *A. vera*, makes a pretty good large container plant.

Ananas. The edible pineapple, which can be a highly interesting, if large, container plant, is in this genus. Often seen in containers is the smaller variety, *A. comosus* 'Variegatus', which has beautiful green-and-white-striped leaves. Be prepared to wait for several years for pineapples to form.

Cotyledon. A most attractive species, *C. undulata*, has felty gray leaves with scalloped edges borne on branched stems, and orange flowers.

Crassula. Many oddities are in this genus of succulents: the jade tree (*C. argentea*), the rosary vine (*C. rupestris*), the airplane-propeller plant (*C. falcata*), and the silver jade plant (*C. arborescens*). All are easy to grow but rather fragile and should be handled with care when moving or shifting.

Echeveria and *Pachyphytum.* The genus *Echeveria* contains many popular succulents, ranging from branching shrubs to ground-hugging rosettes. The leaves are dusted with a waxy bloom that easily rubs off. Some species mimic cacti or jade plants. *Pachyphytum* includes rosette-forming species such as *P. oviferum*, or moonstones, which are irresistible little grayish green plants with fat spoon-shaped leaves coated with a dusty finish.

Euphorbia. The familiar crown of thorns is in this genus, including types with red or yellow flowerlike bracts. Plants are extremely heat-resistant, but do not allow the soil to dry out completely, or the lower leaves will drop. One euphorbia is often confused with cactus: *E. pseudocactus*, an upright, branched plant with stems that have four ribs or wings running their length. All euphorbias have milky juice.

Faucaria. These low-growing gray-green succulents are best known on the West Coast, where they are grown outdoors in protected locations. They form small, fleshy rosettes with hooked spines. Large daisy flowers are a bonus.

Gasteria. Some of the most colorful small succulents are in this genus. *G. maculata* has dark green leaves spotted with white. Wart gasteria (*G. verrucosa*) has tonguelike leaves in a congested rosette, dark green with white warts.

Haworthia. These are little beauties that you can tuck in among larger species. The pearl plant (*H. margaritifera*) has plump, densely packed, tadpole-shaped dark green leaves spotted with white warts.

Kalanchoe and *Bryophyllum.* These are very popular genera, because of their attractive foliage and brilliant, long-lasting flowers. The species range from the erect, felty-leaved *K. beharensis* (velvetleaf) to the tiny, purple-edged pussy-ears (*K. tomentosa*). *K. daigremontiana*, or devil's backbone, is often grown as a curiosity because of the plantlets that form along leaf margins.

Sansevieria. Bowstring hemp or mother-in-law's tongue (*S. trifasciata*) is a durable, aggressively spreading succulent. Most cultivars have narrow, upright, swordlike leaves. The lower-growing rosette types, such as 'Golden Hahnii', are, in my opinion, more graceful in containers.

Sedum. This enormous and useful genus contains everything from the late-flowering hardy garden sedums to the coveted donkey's tail (*S. morganianum*), grown in hanging baskets or atop walls where it can cascade.

Senecio. Includes the odd succulent called hot-dog plant (*S. articulatus*). With age, the segmented stems swell to resemble wieners; the gray-green plants branch and are topped with leaves like ivy.

YUCCAS

Neither cacti nor succulents, sun-loving yuccas are included here because they are often grown in combination with cacti under desert conditions. The Spanish bayonet species, *Y. aloifolia*, includes many extraordinary variegated forms. One form, *Y. recurvifolia*, has pliable leaves, and another has swollen, succulent stems. Some eastern species are very hardy.

Trees and Shrubs

Trees and shrubs are long-term investments, worth the time required to find unusually beautiful cultivars; worth the expense of the plant, container, and planter mix; and worth the regular watering and feeding that keep them in prime condition. There is little point in going to the expense and effort of planting an ordinary shrub or tree in a container. In a landscape, an ordinary plant draws no more attention than an ordinary piece of furniture in a furnished room. When you put an everyday plant in a sizable container and elevate it to the best height for display, however, you focus attention on it. You would soon tire of a poor, drab thing. Look a little harder, pay a little more, and get an outstanding performer that will give you pleasure each day of the year.

The plants that are listed below represent only a small and admittedly subjective slice of the inventory at nurseries and mail-order sources. I have not listed such specialized plants as palms, cycads, giant cacti and euphorbias, and tropical trees, because of their limited range. All of the smaller species in these classes grow well in containers.

Your supplier can advise you on the hardiness of cultivars. Hardiness is critical north of Zone 7, but as you go south you begin to see a greater variety of trees and shrubs in containers. The selection continues to broaden through Zone 9 but narrows in southern Florida, where seasonal dryness can stress plants in containers. Low coastal elevations in central and southern California provide almost ideal environments for growing shrubs from all parts of the world.

When it comes to deciding between a tree and a shrub, much depends on the site. If you want to put the plant on a deck, balcony, or rooftop, a tree may be out of the question because of its weight. All but young, small, or dwarf trees require containers of at least fifty-gallon capacity, which weigh hundreds of pounds when filled with wet planter mix. The best site for trees is on a plot of soil where the tree roots can anchor and the thermal effect of the earth can keep the root system from freezing solid. For such sites, a bottomless, stationary container is preferred.

The second best site for a tree is a patio or paved area, which can support the weight of a medium-sized container (but cannot protect consistently against freezing north of Zone 6). Fifteen- to thirty-gallon containers with bottoms, elevated off the ground for improved drainage, are adequate for

Fall color on garden writer Linda Yang's nineteenth-floor Manhattan terrace, with a crabapple in its autumn foliage, the last roses of the season, bright chrysanthemums, and dying impatiens.
PHOTO BY LINDA YANG

small trees and shrubs in such sites. Containers of this size can be tipped onto a heavy-duty handcart and moved if necessary.

TREES
□ □ □

If you have the right site, go for a tree. What a thrill to visit a large nursery, pick out a slow-growing four- to eight-foot tree, have it delivered to your home, and plant it in a container large enough to keep it happy for four or five years! You have exactly the tree you like in a container that complements its shape, color, and texture and that draws attention like a basketball player in a Cub Scout pack. You can train it as a large bonsai or let it assume its natural form. You can leave it in one place or wheel it around. You can decorate it for holidays and parties and hang birdfeeders from its limbs.

But first things first. Before you visit the nursery, go through a checklist. Let's take it for granted that you will tell the nursery that you want a slow-growing tree adapted to your climate. Then you have to decide whether you want a needle-leaved conifer, a broad-leaved evergreen, or a deciduous tree.

If you like conifers, do you lean toward green, silvery blue, gold, or variegated foliage? Do you want a tightly trimmed pyramid shape, an opened-up conical form which lets you see the trunk and limbs, or an asymmetrical, artfully trained shape such as those that lean over the water in a Japanese garden? If you like broad-leaved evergreens such as holly, sweet-olive, or the laurels, do you prefer variegated leaves? How much does winter fruit count in your evaluation? If your taste is for deciduous trees, can winter bark color and texture hold your interest after the leaves have fallen? Will the falling fruit stain your deck or patio?

CONIFERS
□ □ □

If silver-blue conifers are for you, ask your nursery to show you **Hoops' blue Colorado spruce** (*Picea pungens* 'Hoopsii'), the **weeping Atlantic cedar** (*Cedrus atlantica* 'Glauca pendula'), and the **Scotch pine** (*Pinus sylvestris* 'French Blue'). Equally beautiful but with green needles are the **Austrian black pine** (*Pinus nigra*) and the **dwarf Alberta spruce** (*Picea glauca* 'Conica'). Sizable plants of the gray-green dwarf Alberta spruce are quite expensive, because they grow only a few inches each year.

You don't find as much choice in the broad-leaved evergreen trees, nor are they as hardy as the conifers. The tree hollies — *Ilex opaca*, an American native, and *I. aquifolium*, the English holly — make dense conical trees when pinched and trained. The standard varieties have dark green foliage, but you can buy variegated cultivars. In hollies, it takes two to tango: you'll need a male tree to make the female set berries.

Osmanthus fragrans is not as hardy as the hollies but has the advantage of intensely fragrant creamy white blossoms in early spring. The **bay tree** (*Laurus nobilis*) makes a handsome upright tree with large glossy leaves. Its dried leaves are used for seasoning foods. It is not hardy north of lower Zone 7, but some gardeners will go to amazing lengths to keep a favorite plant alive. Rachel Snyder, retired editor of *Flower & Garden* magazine, wrote me:

I have two friends, sisters, who are avid gardeners and who for years have had as the centerpiece of their terrace garden a large potted sweet bay tree. This tree, of course, wouldn't survive winters in the ground over most of the U.S.A., let alone in a pot on a terrace in Kansas City. Its home is a five-gallon pot of durable plastic material, a concession to reducing the weight, which nevertheless totals about a hundred pounds. These ladies have a special hand truck, a two-wheel type, kept just for — and usually with — this tree. Each autumn, they slide the pot onto the carrier and wheel the plant to winter quarters in the garage, where it sits near a window. On mild days they wheel it out to the driveway for fresh air and sunshine.

Formerly, when a drastic plunge of temperature was forecast, they rolled the tree through a side door into their house, where it rested through the coldest interval on a landing of the basement steps. Now the tree is so big it will not go through a door, so they are heating their garage for it with two oil-fired radiator heaters. Finally, in spring, it goes back to the terrace, with the dolly kept handy in case of need. All the while, this tree is regularly watered almost as routinely as the cat is fed. In response, it has become a beautiful seven-foot specimen that blooms each spring, having reached its maturity. Without question, it is a part of the landscape of this garden.

DECIDUOUS TREES

□ □ □

Your nursery can show you dozens of cultivars of slow-growing deciduous trees, some of which are hardy as far north as Zone 5. The **Japanese maples** are versatile deciduous trees for containers and will grow in partial shade. Fall colors are outstanding, and one cultivar, *Acer palmatum* 'Sangokaku', has coral-red bark during the winter. You might have more difficulty finding the curiously fascinating **paperbark maple** (*Acer griseum*), valued for its peeling, two-tone bark, and the **vine maple** (*A. circinatum*), often grown in a multiple-trunk form.

The Japanese maples are grown principally for their form and foliage, but many slow-growing deciduous trees are appreciated more for their show of

Large junipers act as a windbreak on a Manhattan penthouse terrace.

PHOTO BY LINDA YANG

flowers, and sometimes for their persistent, showy seedpods. Check out the **golden chain tree** (*Laburnum watereri* 'Vossii'), the **golden rain tree** (*Koelreuteria paniculata*), the native American **smoke tree** (*Cotinus obovatus*), the **pagoda dogwood** (*Cornus alternifolia*), and the **Ben Franklin tree** (*Franklinia alatamaha*). If you are thinking about growing dogwoods in containers, be aware that the native **flowering dogwood** (*Cornus florida*) is prone to disease and insect problems; plant *C. kousa* instead.

In Zones 6 through 8, the native **sourwood** (*Oxydendrum arboreum*) is showy in flower and colors up early in the fall. Grow it in acid soil. The weeping **Japanese snowbell tree** (*Styrax japonica*) and the **Korean splendor stewartia** (*S. koreana*) are seldom seen but beautiful at all stages. Any of the hardy deciduous **magnolias** will do well in containers but present a rather stiff appearance during the winter. Most of the flowering plums, cherries, peaches, and crabapples grow too rapidly for containers.

SHRUBS
□ □ □

Perhaps a shrub is more practical for you than a tree. Maybe you would rather have two or three shrubs in ten- to twenty-gallon containers; they can be moved about more easily than trees and will give you greater variety. Shrubs don't have the clean lines of trees, but they can be trained into pleasing forms, and by exploring the dwarf or compact forms, you can find shrubs that will grow for years without needing a larger container.

CONIFERS
□ □ □

Slow-growing coniferous shrubs come in three sizes: pygmy, compact, and dwarf, in ascending order. The pygmies are so tiny and slow to develop that they are usually planted alone or with equally slow-growing alpines in containers. It would be a mistake to plant them with fast-growing annuals or perennials, which would crowd and overgrow these choice, expensive little jewels. If pygmy conifers intrigue you, check out mail-order sources, which offer many more choices than retailers.

You will find a rich selection of compact and dwarf coniferous shrubs at large nurseries, but have the salesperson point out the slow-growing cultivars. It is easy to confuse a young, small, fast-growing conifer with a slow-growing shrub that is two or three years older but the same size.

Slow-growing compact or dwarf coniferous shrubs are much used by commercial nurseries in making up container gardens. They plant slender, upright, conical forms in the center of large containers, then put the creeping, very low-growing forms near the edges and train them to cascade down. Globe- or drum-shaped conifers are rarely combined with other plants, since they display better on their own.

Several hardy **juniper** cultivars creep and hug the ground. Among the best are the dwarf, trailing, greenish blue *Juniperus conferta* 'Emerald Sea' and the lower-growing *J. horizontalis* 'Bar Harbor', which turns from silvery blue to a bronzy plum color in cold weather. Even lower-growing is the blue-green *J. procumbens* 'Nana', which doesn't exceed two inches in height; it sends out branches that curve like tentacles. **Siberian carpet cypress** (*Microbiota decussata*) develops into a low, spreading plant with foliage similar to that of a juniper; it will tolerate light shade.

The **bird's-nest spruce** (*Picea abies* 'Nidiformis') grows slowly into a rather large, flat-topped shrub. Young specimens look good in low, broad containers that mirror the shape of the plant. The spruces are distinct from the junipers in appearance, and have light green new growth. The **weeping Norway spruce** (*Picea abies* 'Pendula') can be trained to cascade over the rim of a large container.

The shrubby **Swiss mountain pine** (*Pinus mugo* var. *pumilo*) is a familiar dwarf landscape plant. This broad, spreading, slow-growing plant with tan candles of new growth is effective in a square or cylindrical container, grown alone and not pruned. The **dwarf Eastern white pine** (*Pinus strobus* 'Nana') is blue-green and shaggier than *P. mugo*.

BROAD-LEAVED EVERGREENS

□ □ □

Dwarf broad-leaved evergreen shrubs for containers are plentiful. The evergreen **azaleas** and other ericacious plants, such as **mountain laurels** and **pieris**, are naturals where you can water them often and maintain the acid soil they demand. Clipped **boxwoods** are often employed in lines or other patterns. In lightly shaded areas, the **Oregon grape holly** (*Mahonia aquifolium*) will give you trusses of yellow flowers followed by clusters of silvery blue berries.

The **Florida anise bush** (*Illicium floridanum*) is a top choice for Zone 7

A ten-by-ten raised-bed planter features
a Japanese maple and ground-hugging
juniper.

PHOTO BY JIM WILSON

and south. It forms a large plant with fragrant foliage, maroon flowers, and star-shaped fruit. Drought and heat are tolerated by this native. A truly dwarf **nandina**, *Nandina domestica* 'Nana purpurea', has richly variegated purple-green foliage that turns scarlet with the coming of cold weather. It is evergreen, or nearly so, and is not grown for berries.

The ***dwarf Nerium oleander*** cultivars, 'Petite Pink' and 'Petite Salmon', can tolerate dry soil and hot conditions south of Zone 7. All parts of this plant are toxic. Wear gloves when you handle it, and don't grow it if you have children. The semihardy ***Raphiolepis indica*** cultivars ask little care in return for flowering over long periods of time. ***Camellia japonica*** and ***C. reticulata*** hybrids will thrive in containers in southern and western zones; cultivars of ***C. sasanqua*** will overwinter in lower Zone 6.

DECIDUOUS SHRUBS

□ □ □

Your challenge when selecting deciduous shrubs for containers is to find cultivars that work hard year-round. They need to be beautiful in flower, foliage, and form, and should offer extras such as fragrance, attractiveness to butterflies, fall color, brightly colored fruit, and interesting winter form or bark texture. Some species, such as the lilacs, are extravagantly beautiful and fragrant, but after they bloom and during the winter are rather ordinary. Others, such as the cotoneasters, have brilliant berries and neat foliage but don't put on a flowery show. None of the following deciduous shrubs can do all things for all people, but each is strong in at least one area, and sufficiently novel to attract attention.

Amelanchier laevis (serviceberry or shadbush) is a large shrub that flowers in late spring and bears colorful fruit in late summer. Train it to a single trunk and plant annuals around it.

Buddleia (butterfly bush) dies back nearly to the ground during the winter and can be cut back to six-inch stubs. This opens the container for planting with winter and spring annuals. Long purple spikes of summer flowers come on new growth of *Buddleia davidii* 'Nanho Purple'. Plant this dwarf cultivar to get flowers the first year and to attract butterflies.

***Callicarpa bodinieri* 'Giraldii Profusion'** flowers heavily with lavender blossoms; then comes a profusion of tenacious violet-blue berries. A large shrub that sets flowers and fruit on new growth, callicarpa should be pruned heavily.

Corylopsis pauciflora (buttercup winter hazel) breaks out its fragrant, yellow, bell-shaped flowers very early, even before forsythia. Surround it with blue and yellow violas, which bloom at the same time.

Corylus avellana **'Contorta'** (Sir Harry Lauder's walking stick) grows slowly and develops contorted, switchback branches. There's nothing quite like it for winter form. Instead of typical flowers it has pendent catkins, which hang on all winter. Keep close watch on your plant when flower arrangers are present; they covet the branches.

Daphne × *burkwoodii* **'Carol Mackie'** is a small, very hardy shrub with medium green leaves penciled in gold. Terminal rosettes of leaves have central clusters of intensely fragrant pink blossoms in spring, following crimson buds. For its size, this shrub can outperform virtually all others.

Enkianthus campanulatus **'Red Bells'** is a hardy ericaceous plant that bears bell-shaped pink flowers in spring and has brilliant fall color. It is hardy as far north as Boston if planted in an oversize container, set on the ground during the winter, and watered during warm spells.

Euonymus alata **'Compacta'** is one of the most brilliant dwarf shrubs for fall color. Colorful berries, attractive to birds, show as the leaves fall. Insist on the dwarf cultivar; the standard shrub grows to great size.

Hydrangea quercifolia (oak-leaf hydrangea) is a large-leaved, slow-growing, shade-tolerant American native. In late summer it bears large, long-lasting white flower sprays that turn pink as they age. The fall color is highly visible. Buy a plant that is large enough to bloom the first year.

Ilex verticillata **'Winter Red'** is a large native deciduous holly with vivid fall color and persistent big red fruits. Berries come at a young age if the male of the species is present. The male can be several feet away in the landscape.

You could hardly find a better container plant for Zones 7 through 9 than *Lagerstroemia indica,* or crape myrtle. Beautiful bark, lovely flowers, foliage that turns carmine in the fall, and persistent seedpods are a few of its assets. Although standard crape myrtles soon grow too large for containers, you can enjoy the dwarf 'Petites' and the precocious little 'Crape Myrtlettes' in many colors. Weeping crape myrtles are available for large hanging baskets.

Myrica pensylvanica (northern bayberry) is a pest-free, slow-growing, large shrub with aromatic foliage and gray-green berries that are used in candlemaking. A male plant is needed to pollinate the female.

Nandina domestica, an old landscaping standby for Zones 6 through 9, has glossy green foliage on bamboolike canes, followed by huge sprays of oval dark red fruit that hang on all winter. The erect branches are virtually bare at the base, which leaves room for you to surround the shrub with annuals and trailing plants. The new cultivar 'Royal Princess' has finely cut, fernlike foliage.

Sambucus racemosa **'Plumosa Aurea'** seems ready-made for large containers. The lacy leaves are a brilliant yellow and red and are followed by bright red berries. Use bright yellow plants such as this to light up dark corners.

Syringa laciniata, the lace-leaved lilac, is unusual among lilacs for its deeply cut leaves and resistance to heat. With their stubby spires of fragrant lavender flowers, the bushes aren't as showy as some lilacs, but they are more durable.

I should also mention that **roses** make marvelous container plants. The standard hybrid teas, grandifloras, and floribundas are not reliably hardy in containers north of Zone 7. However, the miniatures are amazingly hardy, perhaps because they are often grown on their own roots. The new "landscape" class of roses, including the Meideland series and 'Bonica', are about as hardy as the miniatures, and because they are not pruned heavily, they make more graceful plants than garden hybrids. Rose containers are small enough to move easily and can be set on the ground and banked up with soil to overwinter in Zones 5 and 6.

Tree roses, one with a necklace of pink, in unusually handsome ten-gallon terra-cotta planters.

PHOTO BY THOMAS E. ELTZROTH

CHAPTER 5

Edibles

I GET ALL SORTS OF answers when I ask gardeners why they grow edible plants in containers. Sure, fun is at the top of the list. It's also easy, weeds are no problem, and the containers can be placed where they get the most sun, and can even be moved around as shaded areas move with the seasons. For landless city people and apartment dwellers, containers are, of course, the only way to garden. Experienced gardeners tell me they can

There are wonderful design ideas in this picture, even for those of us who can't match this magnificent wall and balustrade. The pots hold a variety of citrus plants.

PHOTO BY JERRY PAVIA

add nearly two months to the growing season by sheltering containers in early spring and late fall. Thoughtful container gardeners say that more than anything else, they value the control they have over what is sprayed on or fed to their crops. Epicures praise the flavor and crispness of foods grown under optimum conditions and eaten within minutes of harvest.

Vegetables

🌱

In addition to all these reasons, I like the simplicity of container farming. I don't have to work out elaborate plans for succession crops or worry about planting tall vegetables in front of short ones. As space opens up in a container, I just slip in a few seeds or seedlings of whatever can be planted at that time of year. Also, containers of vegetables are like theater in the round. You can place them where they can be enjoyed from all sides, like little verdant islands, or stairstep them for viewing from one side only.

The most successful container gardens of vegetables I've grown were planted in shallow seven-gallon plastic tubs, five-gallon plastic buckets, and thirty-gallon plastic garbage cans. Obviously, I was interested more in performance than in aesthetics. If such containers remind you of Hong Kong plastic flowers, you can always spray-paint them a subdued color with a flat finish. For handsome appearance at modest prices, it is hard to beat molded cellulose fiber containers, especially the ones with waxed bottoms for greater durability. Large terra-cotta containers cost about as much as concrete ones and are fragile. I like concrete containers; they will hold up for years, gradually acquire a patina with age, and may prove cheaper than terra-cotta ones over the long haul. Wooden containers look better than any other kind when planted with vegetables, but you should line them with plastic bags so they don't rot.

The real fun comes in choosing the varieties of vegetables to plant in your containers. I'll forewarn you that few of the unusually colorful varieties are available in retail stores as seeds or plants. You can find the common varieties of red chard and bronzy red lettuce, but not much else. However, several mail-order seed companies offer tremendous choices of colorful vegetables and gourmet varieties. In vegetables, "colorful" and "gourmet" aren't necessarily the same. The colorful varieties are good to eat but usually have

Three metal planter boxes painted in bright colors provide rooftop bloom in spring, and the makings of salad and coleslaw later in the summer.

PHOTO BY LINDA YANG

Ornamental edibles: head lettuce, celery, and onions in a shallow

three-gallon wooden tub.

not been bred for maximum flavor. This is especially the case with the bronze lettuces, as opposed to the green-leaf types. Basically, the colors available in vegetables are shades of green, brown, and red, and purple and yellow.

Some vegetables are as homely as a mud fence. Others, by virtue of their foliage or fruit color, symmetrical leaves, or tidy plant habit, are almost too pretty to eat. Not all of these are adapted to growing in containers, but it is a relatively simple matter to pare the list down to those that are both pretty and compatible with containers. All the leafy vegetables, whether they are grown for fresh use in salads or to be cooked as potherbs, mature rather quickly, are very attractive, and give you a lot of good eating from a small space. The red-tinged lettuces offer color for spring and fall container gardens, but no lettuce grows well during hot summer months — unless you garden where people go to escape hot weather.

You could go crazy just trying to choose among the many **lettuce** varieties suitable for container growing. Lettuce is a rather small, quick-maturing plant, and you can harvest the leaf varieties by taking lower leaves instead of the entire plant. Leaf lettuce grows best from direct seeding in early spring and again in late summer and fall. The plants are frost-hardy when tiny but only moderately so as they grow larger and more tender. Some mail-order companies specialize in gourmet lettuce varieties, and if you have never tasted them garden-fresh, there really is a big improvement in flavor over the store-bought kind. Plant pinches of seeds of several varieties to get a mixture of leaf colors and textures. As a rule, the leaf varieties are easier to grow than the heading types, but the 'Buttercrunch' cultivars have small, tender heads and are not difficult.

Red **Swiss chard** such as 'Rhubarb' makes a beautiful summer vegetable, but the elegant 'Fordhook' variety, with dark green leaves and wide white stems, is attractive in its own right, and has a better flavor and texture than the red. Swiss chard grows for months and can be harvested by snapping off outer leaves. Leaf miners can be a terrible problem in certain areas, though. To minimize damage, use floating row covers until the weather turns warm.

Many oriental vegetables are leafy; all grow well in containers. Some of the **Chinese cabbages** have many large outer leaves and spread to cover a circle two feet in diameter. One experience with refrigerating a three-pound head of Chinese cabbage and eating from it for weeks like a Dogpatch ham should convince anyone of the practicality of smaller heads or greens that can be harvested leaf by leaf. The smaller varieties are more efficient. The little variety 'Lei Choy', which resembles a short Swiss chard, is about the prettiest.

Curly endive is decorative in containers. Low and spreading, a mature plant can span two feet. Sow seeds where they are to grow as a succession crop to follow summer vegetables, to mature just after the first frost. Cold weather sweetens the flavor and reduces the natural but not unpleasant bitterness. I like to cover nearly grown endive with a basket for about two weeks to blanch the heads to chartreuse. Blanching removes the bitterness entirely and makes the plants crisp and tender. You can also plant the heading endive called **escarole**. Blanching decreases its bitterness, too. As endive grows, you can harvest outer leaves without harming the plant.

Leaf or heading **chicory** has great potential as a container crop. It is a cousin to endive and includes the high-priced vegetable called **radicchio**. Standard green-leaf chicory can be grown in the fall like endive; I wouldn't attempt spring seeding, because the plants would mature just in time for summer heat to turn them bitter as gall. The red-and-white radicchio takes longer to mature and requires special handling. In the North and cool West, where temperatures leading up to maturity are cool enough to allow the red pigment to develop, spring crops are possible. But the most colorful heads are of the varieties seeded in late summer, wintered over under loose mulch, and cut back to the ground in early spring so that small, colorful heads will form. Choose your radicchio varieties carefully; they are specific for spring or fall crops.

Spinach is well worth growing in containers because it will come very quickly from seeds sown directly in the fall or very early spring. It does suffer from leaf miner damage, and should be protected by a floating row cover. The cover will also concentrate heat and speed maturity. My favorite variety is 'Melody' hybrid. When you harvest the last of the spinach, have plants of **Malabar spinach**, a heat-loving vegetable, ready to replace it. Botanically, the two are not related; Malabar spinach is more for cooking than for salad use. The red variety trails attractively or can be trained up strings. **New Zealand spinach** is another summer substitute; it can take dry heat, whereas Malabar performs better in humid climates.

Of all the cabbage family members, **kale** is the most satisfactory spring and fall crop for containers. Grow just three to five plants and you can strip off enough lower leaves to make a meal. The tops will continue to form new leaves. After a while the plants will look like umbrellas, with long, bare shafts, but will they produce! All of the blue-green curly kales are pretty. For fall harvest, don't overlook the ornamental kales. They taste surprisingly good when cooked, but are a little chewy when chopped for coleslaw.

Cabbage grows well in containers and comes in green, blue-green, and purple-red. Standard cabbage will astound you with its spread, up to three feet tip to tip. The minicabbages grow to about half that size, but plants are hard to find. The best compromise is to grow standard cabbage plants about two feet apart and begin harvesting them when they are half-grown. Grow three plants in a seven-gallon tub or five per half barrel. You have to be meticulous about preventive spraying with *Bacillus thuringiensis*, a biological insecticide, to keep the determined cabbageworms from making holes in the foliage. My personal choices for flavor and color are the Savoy types, with waffled leaves and a silvery blue-green color. Actually, I consider the Chinese cabbages more suitable for spring and fall container growing than coleslaw-type cabbage. They mature faster, can be eaten at smaller stages, and can be planted more thickly. Use the same precautions against cabbageworms; they like Chinese food too.

Broccoli likes to be grown in containers. You can get a very early start by wrapping the container and plant in clear plastic, leaving a chimney for ventilation. The porous, fertile growing medium will encourage the very fast growth that is necessary to the formation of large heads and, after you cut the central bud, secondary, lateral buds. Broccoli is a cousin to cabbage and even more attractive to cabbageworms, so either be faithful with spraying or be prepared to soak the heads in saltwater to kill critters in hiding. My choice in broccoli is 'Early Purple Head', which turns green when cooked. You'll find it under cauliflower in some catalogues, but I maintain that if it walks like a duck, it is a duck. I think you'd be disappointed with the way regular cauliflower looks in containers; it has a lot of leaves for a relatively small head.

Tomatoes are the leading container vegetable. Miniature kinds can be grown in hanging baskets or one-gallon pots, dwarf varieties in three- to five-gallon containers, and the massive hybrid slicing tomatoes in thirty-gallon garbage cans and half barrels. There is no correlation between plant size and fruit size. You can have small plants with fruits the size of apples or large plants with cherry-size fruits. No support is needed for the smaller plants, but the large-vined tomatoes do much better if trained up. The dinky little wire frames sold as supports are useless for the large-vine hybrids. A better arrangement is a cylinder of steel reinforcing mesh wrapped around a thirty-gallon can. Two four-foot cylinders stacked and wired together, to a total height of eight feet, will give large-vine tomatoes enough support to grow to full size. Be sure to use mesh that is big enough for you to reach through to harvest fruits. With such an arrangement, I once grew two plants of 'Floramerica' in a thirty-gallon plastic garbage can and harvested more than sixty pounds of tomatoes averaging seven ounces each. Even larger yields are commonplace.

Genetic resistance to several diseases is available in modern tomato hybrids. Look for the letters V, F, N, T, A, and L in association with names. These signify resistance to verticillium wilt, fusarium wilt, nematodes, tobacco mosaic virus, the alternaria organism that causes early blight, and septoria leaf spot, respectively. Among the best varieties with multiple resistance are 'Park's Whopper' VFNT, 'Celebrity' VFNT, 'Sweet Million' VNTL, and 'Summerset' VF.

Two tomato relatives make good container plants: ground cherry or husk tomato and the Mexican specialty tomatillo. The felty leaves of ground cherries are beloved by whiteflies, but the plants have graceful descending branches. Tomatillos are rather lanky, awkward, upright plants that look better in short cages.

Peppers are among the most beautiful and productive vegetables for container growing. A single large plant or two of the smaller ornamental or garden peppers can be grown in a five-gallon container. Reclaimed five-gallon plastic buckets are popular for growing peppers, and you can spray-paint them to hide their industrial look. Be sure to drill five or six holes a half-inch in diameter in the bottoms.

The big, blocky stuffing peppers are borne on rather bulky, congested-

The salad course: tomatoes, herbs, and flowers in a two-gallon terra-cotta container.

PHOTO BY THOMAS E. ELTZROTH

Terra-cotta pots filled with herbs and flowers blend beautifully with the old brick in John Saladino's Connecticut kitchen garden.

PHOTO BY PETER C. JONES

A brilliant idea! Bright yellow 'Sweet Banana' peppers (which turn red when they mature) hang over yellow marigolds.

PHOTO BY THOMAS E. ELTZROTH

looking plants that remind me of a closet stuffed with clothes. The wedge-shaped salad peppers such as 'Gypsy' hybrid look prettier, grading from green to yellow and finally to red. Virtually all the ornamental peppers are hot; you can choose varieties that turn from yellow when young to red at maturity or from purple to red. The most fantastic ornamental pepper I ever saw is 'Jigsaw', which has leaves flecked with purple, white, and green and glossy dark purple fruits. The most handsome pepper I ever saw, though, was a genuine 'Tabasco' hot pepper grown at Callaway Gardens in Pine Mountain, Georgia. 'Tabasco' needs plenty of heat to mature. Gourmet cooks are trying all sorts of esoteric (for us) varieties of hot peppers in Mexican and Caribbean dishes; these plants have a better chance of succeeding in containers than in a garden.

Planted in the earth, **eggplant** looks homely. But put it in a container and a single plant can become the centerpiece of your garden. One plant can reward you with up to a dozen fruits, which is about all one family can eat without coming to dread the sight of them, in any disguise. Growing eggplant in artificial soil eliminates the serious problem of soil-borne disease. Early in the life of the plants, protect them with a square of floating row cover, or flea beetles may hop on the leaves and reduce them to lace. Once the leaves have been disfigured, there is nothing to do but prune them off.

Purple eggplant comes in all shapes from nearly round to teardrop, including long and skinny like a loofah. My choice is a white variety, 'White Beauty', which is never bitter when harvested young. Don't confuse this cultivar with the inedible ornamental white eggplant called 'Easter Egg'.

Most beans and peas are neither practical nor sufficiently ornamental for container growing. You need several plants to harvest enough for a meal, and they bear for a relatively short time. Two exceptions are **scarlet runner beans** and **hyacinth beans** (*Dolichos lablab*). You can plant several seeds in a ten- to twenty-gallon container and run up strings to a central pole, or string them up to the eaves. By utilizing the space above a container with twining vines, you can harvest enough to make the project worthwhile. Scarlet runner beans and their white-seeded counterpart, 'Dutch Case Knife', make handsome climbers. The pods are tender, stringless, and free of fiber at young stages. Hyacinth beans are more for show than for the pot, but the very young purple pods, shaped like limas, are good to eat.

None of the so-called vine crops — summer and winter squash, pumpkins, cucumbers, and melons — make efficient container plants. They transpire huge amounts of water from their large leaves. Don't get me wrong; they will grow and produce fruit in containers, but they are so large and subject to wind breakage that it is hard to keep them pretty. The best varieties are the dwarf and compact types, which are smaller and less athletic than the standard varieties. If appearance is secondary, the **bush summer squash** are a good bet, and are more efficient than the bush types of winter squash. **Cucumbers** are even more efficient, especially the gynoecious types, which have a preponderance of female blossoms. The muskmelon hybrids with compact vines are marginally productive, and you have to water them so often that the flavor is insipid. Watermelon and pumpkin vines grow so long and require so much water that I consider them hopeless as container plants.

Some of the root vegetables make excellent container plants, and some don't. **Kohlrabi**, especially the purple type, is the hands-down winner for efficiency and beauty. **Radishes** are pretty, and are ready in about four weeks from seeding. **Carrots** grow fast in shallow seven-gallon foot tubs, and taste good. **Green onions** or scallions from sets can be grown close together and make good use of space in containers. Neither will win a beauty contest for foliage, so they are usually interplanted among more attractive, leafy vegetables. Parsnips, rutabagas, celeriac, salsify, and rooted parsley have large plants in comparison to the harvest of edible roots, and need months to mature. They aren't practical at all.

Carrots look pretty seeded around larger, erect plants such as broccoli or tomatoes. You can thin and eat them when they are about the size of your index finger, and leave just a few to grow to full size. Carrots will grow quickly and form smooth roots in planter mixes, if you don't goof and put rough, coarse organic matter in it. They'll come out looking like mandrake roots if you do. Only a few carrot varieties are sweet and full-flavored when young; try the ball-shaped 'Planet' or the tapered 'Minicor'. Direct-seed carrots where they are to grow; they don't transplant worth a hoot.

Unlike carrots, the pretty part of radishes is below ground. The tops look like small, hairy turnip greens. However, radishes do mature faster than most vegetables, and they love the porous soil of planter mixes. In early

Marigolds coexist cheerfully with a
handsome eggplant at the suburban
Victory Garden in Lexington,
Massachusetts.

PHOTO BY JIM WILSON

spring, scatter seeds among larger, slower-maturing vegetables, and pull the plants for roots in four to five weeks. Here's a suggestion: try the much larger winter radishes in containers. Direct-seed them in late summer and set the container in a protected place when hard frost is predicted. Harvest the large roots in early winter. Try the oriental daikon (which is a class rather than a variety), 'Celestial Rose', or 'Round Black Spanish'.

Potatoes — we call them Irish potatoes in the South, to distinguish them from sweet potatoes — make interesting if not terribly efficient container plants. I can't taste any difference between homegrown potatoes and those from the grocery, which diminishes their value to me. The way to grow the most potatoes per container is to plant seed pieces on a shallow layer of highly organic soil in a woven plastic laundry basket. As the pieces of tuber sprout and the stems gain in height, add another layer of planter mix, but don't bury the leaves. Repeat the process every two or three weeks until the basket is full of planter mix. Harvest the potatoes by dumping the container when the vines begin to turn yellow. You will find tubers growing from top to bottom within the root ball, and you should get eight or ten good-sized potatoes per plant. If you go to the trouble of growing potatoes in containers, you should try one of the gourmet varieties, such as the yellow kind or fingerling potatoes.

Sweet potatoes are just as productive and far more attractive in containers than Irish potatoes. You can buy plants of bush varieties, which spread to cover a circle three to four feet across. Plant the rooted cuttings, called slips, two or three per ten- to fifteen-gallon container, and raise it three or four feet off the ground. The vines will trail and grow so abundantly that they will hide the container. Harvest the sweet potatoes just before fall frost, handling them carefully to avoid scarring or bruising, and store them in a very warm, well-ventilated room for curing.

Peanuts are not just an oddity when it comes to container plants. They grow well in five- to seven-gallon containers and make mounded, cloverlike plants with yellow blossoms. If you sprinkle a few teaspoons of limestone over the surface of the soil when you see the first blossoms, the corkscrewing "pegs" that tip down from the blossoms will penetrate the soil and form plenty of goobers. Peanut plants are as ornamental as many flowers, easy to grow from seeds, and quite productive. Although they do best where summers are long and warm, they will grow in the North if you place containers to benefit from heat and sunlight reflected from walls or fences.

If you were to ask me to name the vegetable that returns the most value for your investment and time, I would have to say scallions grown from sets. They grow quickly, can be spaced close together, can be pulled over a long time, and can be interplanted among larger vegetables in containers. You can plant onion sets at any time except midsummer, but they are hard to find except in the spring and fall. Sets are not usually sold by variety, but come in red, white, or yellow — the color of the skin when the scallions begin to mature into onion bulbs. One variety that has to be grown from seeds makes a scallion with ruby-red skin. It is called 'Santa Clause'. (That is not a typo. Clause is the name of a French seedsman.) Surprisingly, you can grow gourmet shallots just as easily as scallions by planting cloves from the clustered bulbs you buy from produce stands.

Herbs grow well in containers, and since you need only snippets of each, they never look gap-toothed or whacked back as garden vegetables can. Some herbs, especially the basils, grow surprisingly large, so forget about putting them in small pots. Collections of herbs in various sizes and designs of pots look especially good in container gardens. Terra-cotta pots display herbs well, particularly those with silver or gray foliage.

My choices for beauty in containers would be **rosemary** (both the erect and the creeping type), the shrubby **Mexican oregano** (*Lippia graveolens*), **lemon verbena**, lemon or oregano **thyme** as a trailer, and **parsley** for hanging baskets. The mounding plants of the small-leaved, compact varieties of **sweet basil**, such as 'Spicy Globe', look good in planter boxes.

One of the best ways to grow herbs in containers is to combine the water-holding capacity of large, shallow containers with the root-restricting action of rather small pots, as Leonard Besser did at the Staten Island Botanical Garden. For example, fill a large, well-drained terra-cotta basin halfway with planter mix. Set three to five clay or pressed fiber pots of six- to eight-inch diameter on the layer of soil and fill them with planter mix. Plant the pots

Herbs and Edible Flowers

HERBS

with herb seedlings, placing the erect kinds in the center. Fill around and over the pots with long-fiber sphagnum moss to hold and evaporate water to keep the plants cool.

In our commercial herb-growing operation, Jane and I have used pots ranging from one to twelve gallons in capacity. Every kind of herb soon grows right out of the one-gallon pots; the plants become rootbound and won't recover when fed and watered. Three-gallon pots do pretty well, but the five-gallon size is best for all sorts. I found the twelve-gallon container heavy and cumbersome, and plants grew slowly in their early stages because the soil was slow to warm up and drain. Even though plastic pots are not as pretty as clay ones, I prefer them, or the flexible four- to six-mil black plastic "nursery bags." These don't have to be watered as often, and they fill out to a square shape, which discourages roots from circling around the bottom. If you want to pretty-up your place for a party, you can slip the plastic bags inside a slightly larger, decorative container.

Herbs with a mounding or trailing growth habit grow quite well in planting towers, planting walls, hanging baskets, large strawberry jars, and spherical or basin-shaped hanging planters lined with sphagnum moss. They look much better than the erect herbs, such as sweet basil, which look awkward and droopy when plugged into the side of a container.

Even if you have space for **mint** in your garden, containers are the place for it — and for other invasive ornamental herbs, such as **artemesia, horehound, catnip,** and **lemon balm**, which, let loose, can take over. All the mints grow well in rather shallow five- to seven-gallon containers, and, except for orange bergamot mint, are among the most winter-hardy of plants. Herbs that drop hundreds of seeds and become pests in the garden also make ideal container plants; **anise hyssop, lemon basil, chamomile,** and certain **artemisias** are just a few of them.

Even when they are small, seedlings or rooted cuttings of herb plants assume the shape they will carry for life; erect, mounded, or trailing. This helps you place erect or mounded herbs in the center and trailing types on the perimeter of large containers. Certain erect herbs, particularly rosemary, can be trained into a tree form with a single trunk, to leave more room for low-growing herbs in the same container.

Herb preference is a matter of personal taste, but sweet basil is by far the

Step up to an herb garden with one- to three-gallon containers of scented geraniums, santolina, rosemary, parsley, and sage.
PHOTO BY GEORGE TALOUMIS

Food at your fingertips: vegetables in
planter boxes surround a raised deck.

PHOTO BY GARY MOTTAU

BLUEBERRIES
□ □ □

Blueberries, one of the so-called bush fruits, make excellent container plants: attractive in flower, fruit, and fall foliage, highly productive, compact, and relatively problem-free. They are one of the ericaceous or acid-loving plants. They can be grown in regular planter mixes but do better in mixes formulated for azaleas, without limestone. They should be fed with fertilizers that leave an acid residue, those branded "azalea-rhododendron food." You can grow blueberries in hard-water areas, but you will have to flush the soil occasionally to avoid a build-up of alkalinity.

Blueberries come in bush, highbush, and rabbit-eye cultivars. The bush cultivars are quite low-growing and are most popular in New England. Highbush blueberries are the choice of commercial producers across the northern states down through Zone 6. Rabbit-eye selections and hybrids with highbush berries do better in the Deep South. Some of the modern blueberry cultivars produce unbelievably large fruits but sometimes at the sacrifice of total yield. Your county Cooperative Extension Service will give you a list of recommended cultivars.

Buy the largest blueberry bushes you can afford, because they have to be two or three years old before they produce enough berries for a meal. With a little care, blueberry bushes in containers will flourish for several years, gaining each year in productivity, beauty, and value.

Fruit Trees

Standard deciduous fruit trees — apples, pears, peaches, plums, apricots, cherries, nectarines, crabapples, figs, persimmons, pawpaws, and such — grow too rapidly for conventional containers. However, you can make attractive containers of cylinders of the wire mesh used for reinforcing concrete; line them with black plastic or with one-by-four treated boards standing on end and wired to the mesh. A cylinder measuring four feet tall by four feet across will hold about fifty gallons of planter mix, an adequate size for starting a standard tree. When the tree outgrows the container, you can strip off the mesh and boards, encircle the root ball with a larger cylinder, and fill in the space with new planter mix or homemade compost. If you make a four-foot-high cylinder five feet wide, it will hold more than seventy-five gallons.

A four-gallon strawberry jar overflowing
with a dozen beautiful plants of
'Sequoia' berries.

PHOTO BY THOMAS E. ELTZROTH

A peach of a combination! The dense
clusters of blossoms on this genetic
dwarf peach will be followed by fruit.
Meanwhile, the simultaneous blooming
of the schizanthus, the two dozen
daffodils, and the peach makes a lovely
spring sight.

PHOTO BY THOMAS E. ELTZROTH

Mesh cylinders lined with boards look good enough for most settings and cost only a fraction as much as conventional containers. When filled, containers of this size weigh a great deal — three hundred to seven hundred pounds — and should be set on the ground. Plants in bottomless containers resting on the ground will survive much colder and drier weather than plants in conventional containers raised on blocks.

You may question the point of planting fruit trees in containers if they are too large and heavy to be moved. Setting small, spreading trees in containers elevates them enough for you to pass beneath the branches, protects the trunk from damage, prevents soil compaction, and provides optimum drainage. In addition, you can plant ornamental or edible plants around the base or chink them into the sides of the container. In short, you can make the space occupied by the tree work a lot harder.

Dwarf fruit trees usually bear earlier, mature at half the size of standards (or less), and can be grown in medium-size containers. To produce dwarf trees, growers graft desirable scion wood onto a hardy rootstock that has been especially selected for slower growth of the top and the root system. Certain dwarfing rootstocks greatly restrict growth, but extreme dwarfs lack winter hardiness in containers.

More dwarfed varieties of **apples** are available than of any other species, and they make good plants for thirty- to fifty-gallon containers. Half whiskey barrels can hold them for a few years, then you have to shift them up to larger boxes of treated wood or wire mesh cylinders.

Certain cultivars of **crabapples** are smaller at maturity than standard apples, more the size of large shrubs. They make good candidates for large containers because they are more attractive in bloom than apples, and the fruits can be pickled, preserved, or left on the tree as food for wild birds.

Pears are not the best choice for containers. They grow well but require several years to hit their stride in production. Also, their usual pruned shape is essentially columnar, which makes the topmost fruits difficult to reach.

One of the best of all small fruit trees is the **genetic dwarf peach**, which owes its smallness and slow growth not to grafting but to genetic makeup. The little trees bear surprisingly large, well-flavored fruit. Standard peach trees bear more quickly and heavily than any other species of fruit tree, and you can keep them to a manageable size for four or five years by cutting back the new growth to two or three leaves per twig in late summer. Peach trees are self-pollinating; you need only one tree, although two will give you better pollination and fruit set. Peaches grow best in Zones 5 through 8. Apricots and nectarines demand more good weather than peaches and more often suffer from damage because of late spring frosts or bad weather when pollen is mature. You are better off growing peaches.

Sour or **pie cherries** bear at a young age and are attractive, more widely adapted than sweet cherries, and winter-hardy. Planting a pollinator cultivar as well as your chosen tree will give you good fruit set. As with all other fruit trees, when cherries grow too large for their containers, you can give them to friends with space in their gardens.

People of Mediterranean ancestry don't have to be told that **figs** make fine small trees for containers, especially wire mesh cylinders resting on the ground. Figs are not reliably hardy north of Zone 7. To give them the best protection, cut them back to a height of four or five feet and wrap both the top growth and the container in two or three layers of spun-bonded synthetic landscape cloth in early winter. Figs set fruit on both old and new wood. In the North, you need to save as much old wood as possible, because fruits that set on new wood may not have time to mature before frost.

Without a doubt, the most beautiful deciduous tree when loaded with fruit is the **Japanese persimmon**. This rather small tree has a graceful form and excellent fall color. The large, colorful fruits look like orange lanterns while ripening. Oriental persimmons are hardy through Zone 7 and marginally hardy in protected microclimates in Zone 6. Buy large trees, because they need a few years to build up enough tissue to support fruit crops. Some cultivars are self-pollinating.

Hardy **pawpaws** of the genus *Asimina* bear the same common name as papayas. There the similarity ends. Deciduous pawpaws grow wild in many eastern woodlands from Mississippi to Michigan and are the only fruit tree that will thrive in moderate shade. The trees are large-leaved, usually multistemmed, and grow to a height of twenty feet. However, they begin fruiting when they are much smaller. The pendent flowers are extraordinary, brownish-purple in one species, white in another. Pawpaws show much promise as container plants, especially *A. triloba*, which has edible, banana-scented yellow fruits three to five inches long.

Meyer lemons in ten-gallon terra-cotta containers are set into a semicircular herb garden of germander and lavender. The pots can be moved inside for the winter.
PHOTO BY JERRY PAVIA

Several tropical species are known as guavas; of these, one — the **pineapple guava** (*Feijoa sellowiana*) — is cold-tolerant in Zone 8, widely adapted, and generally well-liked for eating fresh. A large shrub rather than a tree, it has lovely large blossoms and oblong green fruits, two to three inches long, that are ready around Christmastime and just the right size for scooping out with a spoon. The **strawberry guava** (*Psidium littorale* var. *longipes*) is a large, frost-tender shrub that produces small, vitamin-rich dark red fruits for preserving.

Not related to the garden tomato, the **tree tomato** (*Cyphomandra betacea*) makes an excellent large, quick-bearing shrub for containers. The fruit is shiny, oblong, orange-red, rich in pectin, and used for pies and preserves. The felty leaves are as large as those of southern magnolias.

Papayas make productive, if not particularly handsome, frost-tender tropical trees for very large containers of seventy-five-gallon size and up. They fruit precociously and last for three to four years. Self-pollinating cultivars are available.

Choosing among edible and ornamental plants for containers is not an either/or situation. Most edible plants are attractive, if not truly beautiful — and they have the element of surprise. People are so accustomed to seeing ornamentals in containers that coming upon an attractive container plant loaded with edible leaves or fruit is a delightful and memorable experience. Your standing as a gardener will go up a notch, because visitors will see you as a person who knows plants well enough to venture beyond the pedestrian ornamentals to find dual-purpose edible ornamentals.

Citrus trees need generous containers. This 'Washington Navel' orange thrives in a half barrel.

PHOTO BY THOMAS E. ELTZROTH

III

THE CARE AND
FEEDING OF
CONTAINER PLANTS

Signs of spring: variegated tulips, primulas, and pansies are a
splendid complement to the bright blue doorway.

PHOTO BY DON NORMARK

A container gardener shifts up primulas
from four-inch pots to two-gallon
containers for spring color.

PHOTO BY DON NORMARK

CHAPTER 6

Potting Soils and Planter Mixes

The man who first concocted artificial soils for growing plants must have felt like Icarus when he sensed the growing heat of the sun. Tinkering with something as basic as soil is like flying in the face of nature itself. Hasn't good old garden soil been producing plants since the beginning of time?

Yes, it has, but that was before gardeners began growing plants in containers. Squeezing root systems into small spaces created problems that took years of research to overcome. Horticultural scientists finally did it by mixing various formulations of organic matter and inert material, limestone and starter fertilizers, to perfect what are sometimes called artificial soils or growing media. Producers of the bagged materials you see in nurseries call them potting soils and planter mixes. By whatever name, they are ideal for growing plants in pots and larger containers — far better than garden soil.

These mixes work better than soils because they are lighter and less dense; they absorb more water more quickly, yet they drain better. Being porous, they promote higher oxygen levels in the root zone. They are virtually free of disease-causing organisms and weed seeds. They do not shrink away from the walls of containers when dry and are clean and sanitary to handle.

Some artificial soils are best for growing plants in small pots, and others are more suitable for those in large containers. Although they are labeled in various ways, the knowledgeable gardener can choose the right mix by paying attention to its ingredients and general appearance.

Potting soils are finer in texture than planter mixes. They are made up mostly of peat moss and vermiculite (see below). Some contain relatively small percentages of finely pulverized pine or fir bark as a substitute for part of the peat moss. With their higher percentage of "fines," they hold more water than planter mixes. They are usually sold in smaller packages and are more expensive than planter mixes, and thus are rarely used for filling containers larger than six or eight inches in diameter.

Planter mixes are comparatively coarse blends of finely ground composted pine or fir bark and peat moss. Lightweight, faster-draining mixtures are made by adding perlite (see below). Heavier, denser, slower-draining mixtures are made by adding sand or flame-sterilized topsoil. The speed of drainage can be altered by changing the average size of particles in the mix; the better processors are careful to maintain uniform standards of porosity from batch to batch. They also add limestone to all mixes except those labeled for acid-loving plants such as blueberries and azaleas. Planter mixes usually include minute amounts of nitrogen, so that nitrogen drawdown, created when bacteria rob nitrogen from the soil for their metabolic processes, does not cause deficiencies of this element.

All planter mixes and potting soils are compromises. If mixtures are too fine in texture, they hold so much water that oxygen can't permeate the root ball, and root-rot organisms can take hold. If they are too porous, they can't hold enough water and they dry out rapidly.

Nevertheless, ready-made mixes make your job as a gardener easier and give fairly predictable results. If you start with high-quality mixes and healthy plants, you will seldom lose a plant to root rot. Artificial soil is ideal for container gardening because of the properties of the materials used and their predictable interactions with water, fertilizers, oxygen, and organisms.

Basic Ingredients of Artificial Soils

Sphagnum peat moss is the premium source of fine-textured organic matter for potting soils and planter mixes. Brown and rather chunky, it absorbs and retains a lot of water. High-quality peat moss is virtually sterile and quite acid, usually around pH 4.0 to 4.5. Peat moss naturally contains small amounts of micronutrients but few or no major nutrients.

During recent years, finely pulverized or ground **pine bark** or **fir bark** has become a major ingredient in mixes used by commercial growers for producing nursery stock in containers, and processors use it as the major ingredient in planter mixes for outdoor containers. It costs less than peat moss and works almost as well. *Almost* is the key word; most growers still incorporate sphagnum peat moss in their mixes for greater water absorbency and for its finer consistency.

Regular-grade ground bark is produced by hammer-milling the sawmill by-product, spraying it with a nitrogen solution, and piling it for composting. The highest-quality material is made by grinding the composted product again and piling and aerating it for additional composting. Double grinding and composting produces a product that seldom causes nitrogen drawdown and yellowing of plants.

Vermiculite, also sold as Terralite, is mica that has been "popped" under heat and pressure. It is completely sterile and very water-absorbent, yet because of its rather large, flaky particles, it is quicker to drain than peat moss. It is usually neutral in pH and contains small amounts of potash. You can recognize vermiculite by its glittery gold and silver particles.

I like vermiculite in potting soils but don't use it in mixtures for large containers, because the fluffy particles are fragile and can collapse and compact if the container is moved or jostled. Also, vermiculite holds so much water that it adds appreciably to the wet weight of mixes.

Of all the materials used in planter mixes to make them lighter and faster-draining, **perlite** is the best. This is a gritty white material with particles of various sizes. Perlite doesn't absorb water, but it does hold a certain amount on its rough surfaces. It is sterile and nearly neutral in reaction. The only drawback to perlite is its tendency to blow away when it is washed to the surface by watering. Potting soils rarely contain perlite because it makes them drain too fast.

Composted milled sawdust is sometimes used as a component of regular-grade planter mixes. It is a good, relatively coarse material but breaks down faster than ground bark. As the particles oxidize and diminish in size, the mix settles, becomes denser, and drains more slowly. This is why you should use composted sawdust in moderation.

There was a time when processors routinely added **topsoil** to artificial mixes, because (among other reasons) it was cheap. No more: a few developers still scalp the topsoil from residential developments and sell it, and a few farmers will sell their topsoil, but the practice is disappearing.

The "other reasons" are horticulturally sound. By including perhaps 10 to 15 percent sandy loam in mixes, processors can increase the water- and nutrient-holding capacity of the mix and reduce the likelihood of nutrient — especially micronutrient — deficiencies. Sometimes the label on a mix will tell you that topsoil is included. You are more likely to find topsoil in potting soils than in planter mixes.

Commercial growers routinely add **sand** to mixtures, to gain the weight necessary to keep tall container-grown plants from toppling over. But mixes for home gardeners contain sand for another reason as well: to reduce production costs. The cheaper mixes may contain so much sand that they are dense and slow to drain. A friend in the bark-processing business suggested a good home test for porosity: fill a six-inch pot with the mixture, tap it down lightly, and pour a quart of water through it; if all the water filters through in less than a minute, the porosity is about right.

If you notice broad-leaved weeds or grass coming up in containers of planter mix, switch to a premium brand. In all probability, the processor used river sand polluted with weed seeds or a product aptly called **muck**. Muck contains organic accumulations dredged from ponds and streams; it is often infested with weed seeds and is so fine in texture that it makes mixtures drain poorly.

Many gardeners associate black color with fertility in soils, but this holds true only for garden soil, not for the artificial soils used for growing plants in pots or containers. High-quality sphagnum peat moss is brown, not black. Composted ground bark is black but contains very few nutrients except for the nitrogen that is added during the composting process. Muck is black as pitch but is to be avoided. Vermiculite is golden or silvery; perlite is white. Consequently, you should ignore color when choosing a mix.

The only reliable guide to the quality of a mix is the reputation of its processor. Some brands of high-grade planter mixes and potting soils you are most likely to find in stores include Peters, Pro Gro, Jiffy Mix, Redi-Earth, Ball Peat-Lite, Metro-Mix, Flower Power, Lambert, Baccto, Hyponex, Touchstone, and Fafard. I recall a good planter mix on the West Coast branded Silver Spade. In the East I often see the Hoffman and Plantation Professional Growers brands.

Additives for Artificial Soils

Although the packaged mixes used as is will grow a wide range of plant species, you can add a number of things to make them work better. It is safe to assume that the processor will have added enough limestone to raise the pH of the mix to the range of 6.0 to 6.5 (except for azalea mixes) and to supply calcium and magnesium for three or four months. And you can assume that the nitrogen applied during the composting process will run out after three or four weeks. Therefore, you will probably be starting with a mix that contains little or no phosphorus or potassium, only a trace of nitrogen, few micronutrients, and only a short-term supply of calcium and magnesium. Biological activity will be low at first but will increase with time.

Planter mixes can benefit from additional calcium. You can add **gypsum** as a source of this secondary plant nutrient without changing the pH of the mixture. About one-half ounce per gallon should be sufficient; mix it in thoroughly. Add **superphosphate** at the same rate to improve the speed of rooting and the strength of the root system. To improve water retention, you can add a **polymeric water absorbent** such as Water Grabber, HydroSource, Supersorb, Plant-A-Gel, Aqua-Grow, and Gel-Scape. These inert materials are not toxic to plants. They increase the water-holding capacity of mixes without significantly decreasing the speed of drainage or the aeration. **Controlled-release fertilizers** such as Osmocote or Nutricote will feed plants over an extended time (see Chapter 7). With each product, follow the directions on the package.

To increase the weight of the mixture, you can add sand or **calcined clay**, which resembles fire-glazed kitty litter. The clay is superior to sand because it keeps its shape, is virtually inert and sterile, does not decompose or absorb water, and is free of weed seeds. Calcined clay is often used in the production of lightweight cement blocks. If you can't find it through a distributor of greenhouse and nursery supplies, try your local manufacturer of blocks.

Granite dust, sometimes called **granite flour**, is a quarry by-product. It is heavy, but because the particles are so sharp, it does not pack down like sand. It is sterile, does not absorb water, and releases small amounts of potassium as it degrades. Many advanced growers swear by it as an additive for mixes that contain no sand.

Homemade Mixes

As you add containers to your garden, you may reach the point where you feel confident enough to make your own mixes. You can do it rather simply and save your own mixes. You can do it rather simply and save money if you buy the components shrewdly and in large batches. Blend the ingredients in the spring when you are filling a number of containers. Be sure not to add controlled-release fertilizers until you are ready to use the planting mix, because the moisture in the mix will activate the release of nutrients and salts.

As a home gardener, you may find it useful to keep three kinds of mixes (either ready-made or homemade) on hand, and perhaps a fourth for special situations. Buy plastic garbage cans that are the right size to hold a bag of planter mix, and keep the lids on tight to exclude contaminating dust.

SEED FLAT MIX

I'm sorry there is not a better word than *flats* for the shallow little containers used for starting plants from seeds; the name is a holdover from the days when gardeners had to use wooden "flats" or boxes with cracks between the bottom slats for drainage, rather than plastic or aluminum pans. Oh, did we have problems getting seeds started back then, using recycled flats and garden soil, and with only natural light! The soil tended to be cold and wet, and we often lost seedlings to damping-off disease (see Chapter 11), which is more prevalent where the light is weak.

Now, with fluorescent lights and nearly sterile special mixtures, you can coax seeds to germinate quickly and strongly, and seedlings reach transplanting stage with little or no loss to damping-off. These mixes incorporate the best materials and have been specifically developed for starting seeds indoors and growing seedlings for transplanting. I like to use them also for the transplanting of tiny seedlings of expensive varieties to their first small pots, because damping-off can kill seedlings at this stage as well as earlier.

Most people purchase the small amounts of mix they need to start seeds, but if you want to make your own, mix one part coarse sphagnum peat moss with one part sterile horticultural vermiculite. You can pasteurize the peat moss by moistening it slightly, placing it in a casserole dish, and microwaving it on the high setting for three minutes per quart. If you microwave two quarts at a time, stop the process after three minutes, pivot the dish ninety degrees, and heat it for two or three minutes longer. Don't include sand or vermiculite when you microwave, as it can contain metallic particles.

Make up small batches of mix at a time on a clean table. Mix the pasteurized peat moss with the vermiculite and seal it in a container to exclude dust. Don't add limestone or starter fertilizer.

Always use washed containers for starting seeds. If you reuse containers, sterilize them in a 10 percent solution of household bleach. Soak the pots for a while in the solution to soften deposits of salt, then wash them thoroughly. You may have to use a scrubbing brush or pad to remove unsightly encrustations.

Many commercial growers use straight sterile vermiculite to start seeds, and it works fine. But I have trouble regulating the watering of plants in vermiculite, and I've found that seedlings stay in condition longer without fertilization when peat moss and vermiculite are mixed. Also, I like the way that peat particles cling to rootlets when I use a mix. Seedlings pricked out of vermiculite come out easily, with their root systems intact, but the roots are nearly bare.

POT PLANT MIX

■ ■ ■

Use this to fill pots up to eight inches in diameter (one-gallon capacity).

If you grow only a few pot plants, buy a high-quality ready-made mix. However, if you grow large numbers of plants, use the following formula to mix your own. You don't need to sterilize the peat moss, because pot plants are larger, have stronger root systems, and are less susceptible to plant diseases than seedlings. Here's the recipe:

1 part moistened sphagnum peat moss
1 part vermiculite
Pelleted dolomitic limestone, at 1/2 ounce per gallon
Triple superphosphate, at 1/4 ounce per gallon
Gypsum (optional), at 1/2 ounce per gallon

Do not add other fertilizers.

PLANTER MIX

■ ■ ■

Use the planter mix to fill containers that hold one gallon or more, to fill planter boxes, or in raised beds.

You can make relatively cheap, effective planter mixes by combining equal parts of coarse, medium, and fine particles. This formula, which I made up for growing vegetables and ornamentals, works well for a wide range of species:

1 part small nuggets of pine or fir bark, for the coarse fraction
1 part pulverized (ground) pine or fir bark, for the medium-sized fraction
1 part moistened coarse sphagnum peat moss, for the fine fraction (the chunks in it improve drainage)

Mix in pelleted limestone, superphosphate, and gypsum at the rates recommended for the pot plant mix. Also, consider adding polymeric water absorbents so you don't have to water too frequently. (Be sure not to exceed the rate suggested on the package.)

ULTRA-LIGHTWEIGHT PLANTER MIX

■ ■ ■

Use this mix for filling portable containers or for weight-sensitive plantings on balconies, on rooftops, or in windowboxes.

Much of the weight of planter mixes comes from the water absorbed by particles or trapped in the interstices between them. You can reduce weight by incorporating fluffy, feather-light, horticultural-grade perlite. Perlite particles are strong and retain their shape in large containers filled with heavy soil.

Despite the demand for ultra-lightweight mixes, some stores don't carry them because the perlite runs up the price. To make your own, use this formula:

> 2 parts small nuggets of pine or fir bark
>
> 2 parts pulverized pine or fir bark
>
> 1 to 2 parts perlite (if you use 2 parts, be sure to mix in a polymeric water absorbent to increase the water-holding capacity)

Mix in limestone, superphosphate, and gypsum as recommended for the pot plant mix.

Pellets of Styrofoam are sometimes used as a substitute for perlite, but they gravitate quickly to the surface and blow away. Some professional horticulturists mulch large containers with decorative pebbles to protect the Styrofoam or perlite from the wind and to reduce evaporation.

If you follow these recipes, your homemade potting soils and planter mixes should drain readily, yet be neither too dry nor soggy. They should absorb water instantly and thoroughly, with no dry pockets in the root zone. They should decrease in volume no more than 25 percent over a full growing season, and should not require additional limestone unless you recycle them. The quickly available pelleted limestone should prevent blossom-end rot in fruiting vegetables and fruit and berry crops in containers. If dry pockets do develop in your container mixes, you can remedy the situation by watering once a month with a wetting agent called a surfactant, which "makes water wetter" by decreasing the surface tension of water droplets (see Chapter 9).

After you have settled on one or more potting soils and planter mixes and used them successfully for a season, you will begin to feel more secure with them. It is better not to reuse them, because of possible problems from residues, pathogens, and compaction due to alteration of particle sizes. Dump used mixes on your flower garden, or use them to mulch around shrubs and ornamentals.

CHAPTER 7

Fertilizers

You could compare feeding plants growing in artificial soil to feeding infants. Everything they need has to come from you, and on schedule. And just as little children prefer some kinds of food to others, various kinds of plants thrive better on particular nutrients. Unlike babies, though, plants can't shove foods they don't want off a highchair tray.

When feeding plants in containers, you have little margin for error. Artificial soils do not have the same forgiving capacity as good garden loam to neutralize excess fertilizer. With all my experience, I have burned a few container plants with too-strong fertilizers applied when the plants were suffering from drought. The same fertilizer applied to garden soil would not have caused a problem. The difference lies in tiny garden soil particles, mostly clay and humus, that can reduce the shock caused by fertilizer applications. Literally, these negatively charged soil particles attract and hold positively charged nutrient ions. There are

fewer such buffers in artificial soils, which means you must be doubly careful to apply fertilizer exactly as directed on the package.

An old friend, Hollis M. Barron, who has had more than thirty years' experience in plant nutrition, reminded me of another major consideration in feeding container plants. "With garden-grown plants," he said, "the gardener has a greater latitude in where to place fertilizers for maximum safety and utilization, whereas with container-grown plants, you more or less have to cram fertilizers down their throats to get it into their root systems. Together with the generally higher rates of application used in fertilizing container-grown plants, this means you have much less room for mistakes."

Forgive me for bringing up a fertilizer fact that you probably know by heart, but understanding plant foods begins with fertilizer analyses, the information required on labels or tags by state laws. Percentages of the three major plant

[1 7 1]

nutrients, nitrogen (N), phosphate (P_2O_5), and potash (K_2O), are listed on tags and labels in that order, and are generally referred to as "NPK" for the sake of simplicity.

Fertilizers come in several forms, the most common of which are dry granular, water-soluble, and controlled-release.

Dry Granular Fertilizers

These are standard garden, lawn, or farm fertilizers designed to be applied dry to the soil and worked in, or cultivated in alongside rows of plants. Dry granular fertilizers are much less expensive than crystalline or liquid concentrated fertilizers, but for feeding plants in containers they are hazardous, inefficient, and far less predictable. No fertilizer, regardless of its form, is entirely utilized by plants; dry granular fertilizer is perhaps the least efficient, because its nitrogen is subject to volatilization and leaching, its phosphate to fixation in insoluble forms, and its potash to leaching. Only a small fraction of typical "complete" dry granular fertilizers (containing all three major elements) actually dissolves; the remainder breaks down slowly by a process called hydrolysis.

Because of their danger to plants and other shortcomings, I never apply dry granular fertilizers around plants in containers. The only such fertilizer in my storage shed is superphosphate, which I incorporate when making up planter mixes.

Water-Soluble Fertilizers

Water-soluble fertilizers dissolve and go into solution quickly, especially in warm water. Most are formu-

lated from chemical sources, but some are made from fish by-products. Many organic growers who use fish emulsion are not aware that it may have been laced with chemical fertilizers to raise the figures in the analysis; read the label to see whether you are getting only the natural product.

Water-soluble fertilizers are designed for foliar feeding and drenching on the soil around plants: commercial growers call this liquid feeding. Home gardeners can buy very high-analysis soluble fertilizers such as 20-20-20, with a total NPK content of 60 percent. These generally give you a better value than low analyses, which are made milder partly to help beginners avoid burning plants with strong solutions. For example, a fertilizer with the formula 3-3-3 has a total NPK content of 9 percent. You need to use more than six times as much of it to produce the same effect as you get with one application of 20-20-20. Pound-for-pound price comparisons between water-soluble and dry granular fertilizers are misleading; the former are more expensive because they are more difficult to manufacture.

Some soluble fertilizers come bagged or boxed in crystalline forms, whereas others are dissolved in water and are sold in bottles and jugs. Predissolving the fertilizers reduces the total content of active ingredients, but makes them simple to measure with an eyedropper or a measuring spoon. (Be careful with ordinary teaspoons and tablespoons; they can vary in capacity. Use a measuring spoon, and respect the considerable difference between the level, rounded, and heaping measures used in rates of application.)

Directions for application average about one level teaspoon of high-analysis fertilizer per gallon of water, if you feed with every watering. Plants cannot fully utilize stronger solutions, which may not burn plant roots but result in waste. When comparing the application rates of various brands of water-soluble fertilizers, you will see some contradictions and anomalies, which result from varying degrees of caution on the part of formulators.

Keep two formulations of soluble fertilizer on hand for

feeding plants in containers. You will probably have to settle for approximations of the following ratios, since every manufacturer has its own set of analyses.

To feed foliage plants, broad-leaved evergreens, and leafy vegetables all season, and to feed your fruits and fruiting vegetables for the first six weeks of the season, use a fertilizer with a 2:1:1 ratio of NPK — for example, 20-10-10. This gives your plants the generous amount of nitrogen they need without loading them up with excessive phosphate and potash. You could use 20-20-20 fertilizer, and it would work pretty well, but it could increase the risk of salinity damage from too much phosphate and potash. You will see the same application rates listed for 20-10-10 and 20-20-20; this is because nitrogen is the key element. Plants are more sensitive to too much nitrogen than to too much phosphate or potash.

Manufacturers aren't just trying to sell you another package of fertilizer when they recommend a different formulation to feed flowering plants all season or to encourage fruit set after midseason. Flowering or fruiting plants need a fertilizer with less nitrogen and more phosphate and potash. Use a 1:2:1 or 1:2:2 NPK ratio, which translates to a 15:30:15 or 10:20:20 analysis. If you feed flowering or fruiting plants with a high-nitrogen analysis such as 20:10:10, or a "balanced" analysis of 20-20-20, you will give them more nitrogen than they can use. You may not injure or kill them, but you may force vegetative growth at the expense of flower or fruit formation.

Before you apply a liquid fertilizer, water the soil thoroughly to reduce the risk of burning plant roots. Let the excess water drain out, then pour on the fertilizer solution. The preliminary watering will leach out the accumulated salts so the fertilizer won't drive the salinity beyond toxic levels. Every few weeks, water with a solution of horticultural wetting agent (a surfactant) such as Aqua-Gro or Kelo's HydroWet, to moisten stubbornly dry particles.

If you have only a few container plants, make up fertilizer solution a gallon or so at a time and pour it on the soil. However, if you have several plants in containers and wish to feed garden plants as well, you will need a quicker, easier way to apply fertilizers. Consider having an inexpensive siphon device to meter the solution into a water hose. The smallest and simplest siphons are sealed into hose-end applicators which are screwed onto pint or quart bottles. You make up a concentrated solution in the bottle and turn on the water; a siphon action sucks the solution into the hose and meters it at the proper concentration. Another type is simply a brass fitting threaded for a male connection on one end and a female connection on the other, which you connect between a water hose and a faucet; a rubber spaghetti tube drops into a bucket of concentrated fertilizer solution and siphons it into the hose at a 1:16 ratio.

When feeding container and garden plants through a siphon, I make up a concentrated solution of sixteen level teaspoons in a gallon bucket, turn on the hose, and drop the spaghetti tube into the solution. I use crystalline Peters fertilizer, which contains a blue dye, so I can see when the blue color begins to come out of the hose. I can also hear the suction created by the siphon. I know the concentrate is being diluted to one teaspoon per gallon in the water being applied around plants.

The formula of the fertilizer doesn't matter; if you multiply the recommended application rate by sixteen to make up the concentrate, it will come out right when diluted by the siphon.

The only problem with using siphons around the yard is that fertilizer salts can be sucked back into the house water if you don't install a check valve. Most municipalities have ordinances requiring back-flow check valves in water lines where hoses can be connected and used to apply fertilizers, insecticides, or herbicides in solution. The danger that chemicals will be sucked back into drinking water is so real that some Florida towns require two check valves for safety. I have installed two on the water line leading to my greenhouses, so that the backup valve can catch any traces of chemicals that might leak through the first valve.

By the way, when using a hose for liquid feeding, always use up the concentrate and let clear water run through the hose. You never can tell when someone is going to pick up a hose and drink out of it. Weak fertilizer solutions probably won't make anyone seriously ill, but they can cause digestive upsets.

Some gardeners like to use liquid fertilizer solutions for foliar feeding. These are especially good for quickly restoring color to faded foliage and for rectifying iron or zinc deficiencies where the water has a high pH reading. You have to take greater care than when you simply pour the solution on the soil around plants, however. Be very careful when making up the solution, and do not foliar-feed when the sun is high. Certain fungicides and insecticides are compatible with foliar fertilizers; your Cooperative Extension Service has a list.

Controlled-Release Fertilizers

Sometimes called timed-release fertilizers, these measure out nutrient ions over a period of three to nine months. They are of four distinct classes:

1. *Pellets of high-analysis, dry, water-soluble fertilizer coated with a thin layer of plastic.* The plastic forms an osmotic membrane through which nutrient ions are slowly released into the soil. Water penetrates the membrane and dissolves the fertilizer, setting up a different concentration of salts inside the pellet and in the surrounding soil water.

The rate of nutrient release depends almost entirely on soil temperature. Release ceases at about 40°F, when the pores in the membrane close. The nutrient release spans are measured at an average soil temperature of 70°F. For example, a single application of Osmocote 18-6-12, an Ameri-

can-made fertilizer of this type, will feed for eight to nine months at an average soil temperature of 70°. By comparison, the Osmocote 14-14-14 formulation, which has a thinner, more porous plastic coating on the pellets, will feed for three to four months. Recommended application rates of Osmocote may seem very high, but the pellets must feed plants for several months. The plastic coating prevents them from burning plant roots when applied as directed.

You won't find Osmocote pellets included in ready-made potting soils, because the soils are moist: after about a week, the moisture would start the nutrient-release process, and ammonia and salts could build up to a harmful level. For the same reasons, don't add Osmocote to your home-made artificial soils until just before use.

If you have a choice between top-dressing with Osmocote and incorporating it into the soil, mix it with the soil. When surrounded by soil particles, the coated pellets will remain uniformly moist, and the rate of release will be constant. In contrast, the alternating wetting and drying of exposed top-dressed pellets will slow down the rate of nutrient release. Reapplications of Osmocote on long-term container plants should be mixed into the surface of the planter mix for improved efficiency.

If you are striving to achieve the maximum rate of growth for your container plants, consistent with good production of flowers or fruit, consider a feeding program advocated by several universities. Incorporate Osmocote in the soil at half the recommended rate and supplement it with liquid feeding at half rate. Feed with every watering, but use clear water every week or so.

2. *Granules that hydrolyze and break down slowly.* MagAmp, a high-phosphate fertilizer, is in this class. It is magnesium ammonium phosphate, fortified with potash. An inherent disadvantage of this kind of fertilizer is that the rate of release of the three elements is not the same, depending more on the amount of moisture passing over the surface of the granules than on soil temperature. MagAmp per-

forms best in warm, biologically active soils, where its ammoniacal nitrogen is readily converted to the nitrate form available to plants. It is more often mixed with artificial soils than applied as a top-dressing.

3. Granules that decompose to release nitrogen. Ureaformaldehyde, which is about 42 percent nitrogen, is in this class. Referred to colloquially as UF, it contains only nitrogen, and has long been used to extend the release of nitrogen in lawn fertilizers and slow-release fertilizer tablets. The speed at which nitrogen is released depends on the activity of nitrifying bacteria in the soil. A uniform release rate depends on warm, well-aerated soil with good moisture content. One convenient fertilizer containing UF as the nitrogen source is Agriform 14-4-6; the tablets contain a dispersant, so that when you place them on the surface of soils in containers and flood them with water, they break down into granules.

UF is a good fertilizer to add to homemade artificial soils containing raw wood products, because it can reduce nitrogen drawdown over an extended period. The release of nitrate nitrogen in container soils is slow at first, but increases as the population of nitrifying bacteria builds up in the root zone and begins to convert nitrites into nitrates. Commercial nursery growers mix about two pounds of UF with each cubic yard of artificial soil.

4. Granules that are coated with molten sulfur to slow down the release of nitrogen. Sulfur-coated urea is an example. Originally limited to supplying extended-release nitrogen for lawn fertilizers, this substance is now being included in garden fertilizers. The release rate of urea, a nitrogen source, depends on the slow degradation of the jacket of sulfur on the granules. While not precise, the release mechanism represents a distinct improvement on standard dry granular nitrogen sources. I expect to see more sulfur-coated urea used in formulations for feeding container plants, because it provides extended release of nitrogen at relatively low cost per pound.

Organic Sources of Plant Nutrients

Fertilizers made from animal or vegetable by-products are preferred by organic gardeners. However, the most popular organic nutrient sources — blood meal, tankage, "blood and bone," feather meal, soybean or cottonseed meal, manure, and composts fortified with manure — are not water-soluble. All of these break down and release plant nutrients under the action of soil organisms, which are not abundant in planter mixes and potting soils and which are virtually inactive in cold soils. With the coming of warm weather, organic fertilizers can release a surge of ammonia and make the root zone too "hot" for the comfort of plants in containers.

I have experimented with feeding container plants with dry organic materials — cottonseed or soybean meal, for example, dressed on the surface of the planter mix and swirled in. But these fertilizers tend to putrefy and generate a smell that is too "organic" for even this old farmer.

Some organic gardeners solve this dilemma by feeding plants with manure tea, made by suspending a cloth bag of barnyard manure, composted stable litter, or chicken, rabbit, or cricket manure (see below) in water. In a few days, nitrogen and some potash are liberated by the action of bacteria in the water, and the dark "tea" can be poured around plants. The brew also contains organic compounds such as amino acids, enzymes, and perhaps vitamins, which can be broken down and absorbed by plant roots, but the major direct benefit of manure tea comes from the nitrogen component.

I conducted some greenhouse tests to find the best way to feed large container plants after the Osmocote in the soil ran out. I found that these older plants benefited from occasional feedings with organic fertilizers in addition to regular feeding with high-analysis water-soluble fertilizers. I fed them with a tea made from, of all things, cricket manure. A friend has a bait farm, which produces billions of crickets for fishermen, and the little critters create quite a pile of manure, dry and not unpleasant-smelling. It is lower in analysis than chicken manure but is nearly free of weed seeds.

To make manure tea, I put ten pounds of dry cricket manure in a cloth bag and suspend it in a thirty-gallon plastic garbage can full of water. After three or four days in the warm greenhouse atmosphere, the tea begins to smell. I slosh the bag up and down a few times to liberate as much of the strong solution as possible. Then, using two five-gallon plastic buckets, I dilute one part tea with four parts water. I use up all the tea, then refill the barrel with water to make another batch with the original manure. This gives me enough for a couple of waterings, then I go back to feeding with manufactured fertilizers for a while. Invariably, I see a burst of new growth a week or so after applying manure tea. I use the spent manure as a mulch around garden plants.

I can't explain why the cricket manure tea produces a rush of new growth in container plants that have been regularly fed at high rates with water-soluble manufactured fertilizers. It probably supplies something that is missing in chemical fertilizers — complex organic compounds and bacteria that assist in converting mineral nutrients to forms usable by plants.

You can't just run down to the store and buy cricket manure, but you can get good results with teas made from other animal manures: sheep, rabbit, horse, cow, or chicken. Whatever you use will result in a tea that will differ from mine, so you will have to find a safe, effective concentration by trial and error. Just remember that certain plants are especially sensitive to fertilizers, even organic ones, and to the ammonia in manure teas. Ferns, azaleas, orchids, and ericaceous plants such as azaleas and rhododendrons are notably sensitive, and certain bedding plants, such as impatiens, can become too "growthy" with manure tea, at the expense of blossoms.

All manure teas work better on outdoor container plants after the soil has warmed in the spring. I'm afraid to use them during the winter because of the possibility that ammonia will burn roots in the cold soil.

An easy but more expensive way to feed container plants organically is to feed them with fish emulsion diluted in water according to directions. As with the manure teas, nitrogen is the most important component of fish extracts.

If you prefer to grow container plants organically, you should be sure to incorporate in your planting mix some dolomitic limestone, plenty of rock phosphate or colloidal phosphate as a source of phosphorus, greensand or granite dust to supply potassium, and a little blood meal to overcome the initial nitrogen drawdown. Topping these mixed-in ingredients with regular feedings of manure tea should produce excellent plants. I would suggest mixing into each cubic foot of artificial soil

- 4 ounces dolomitic limestone, to correct the pH and supply calcium and magnesium
- 1 pound rock phosphate or colloidal phosphate (these sources of phosphorus are not nearly as concentrated as superphosphate)
- 4 to 6 ounces greensand plus 1 pound granite dust
- 2 ounces blood meal (no more, because ammonia-forming nitrogen will be liberated quickly in warm soil).

All of these materials are considered acceptable by most organic gardeners. This combination of additives can prevent or greatly reduce three of the most troublesome problems that can occur with organically fed container plants: a profound shortage of calcium and magnesium, which results in stunted, bleached plants; blossom-end rot of fruiting vegetables and bush or tree fruits (which is also aggravated by moisture stress); and nitrogen drawdown.

Whether you grow plants with organic or chemical fertilizers, I can't stress too highly the necessity of fortifying artificial soils before filling containers. When making up planter mixes or potting soils, I always use pelleted limestone instead of ground limestone, because the latter is like coarse sand and breaks down slowly. Pelleted limestone is made by rolling powdered limestone into little balls. In the presence of soil moisture, the pellets disintegrate into powder, which presents much more surface area and can neutralize soil acidity faster. The readily available calcium and magnesium helps to prevent blossom-end rot, which starts when a shortage of these elements causes root hairs to deteriorate and the plant can no longer take up enough water.

Nitrogen drawdown occurs when the raw organic matter in artificial mixes is attacked by bacteria that need nitrogen to complete their metabolic processes. They will steal it from plants if you don't supply it as a fertilizer. Nitrogen drawdown is manifested by stunted, yellowish plants. It may reoccur several weeks into the growth cycle of container plants, when the initial effect of additives wears off. If you see it happening, feed more frequently and add some organic nitrogen to stimulate the growth of helpful bacteria in the artificial soil.

Variables in Fertilizing

Feeding plants is part science, part art. The concept that it is a precise science, not an art, doesn't hold up in practice, at least not for home gardeners. Several factors can complicate your calculations.

First, some of the components of artificial soils contain nutrients. Peat moss contributes a bit of nitrogen as it decomposes, vermiculite contains potassium, and loams contribute the three major elements plus calcium, magnesium, and sulfur. Nevertheless, in practice you should feed as if the plants were growing in pure nutrient-free sand, because

they are able to absorb some nutrients beyond their actual needs.

Second, a significant amount of nutrients will be lost in drainage water. Good practice requires that you apply water until some runs out of the drainage holes. The loss, especially in nitrogen and potash, is unavoidable. Some nitrogen will also be lost to volatilization; that is, it will escape into the air as a gas.

Third, tap or well water used for irrigating can contain nitrogen in the nitrate form, plus secondary nutrients and micronutrients. A more serious concern, however, is hard water, in which calcium, magnesium, and sodium are present in excessive amounts. You may have to water liberally to wash away dissolved salts. In some areas, extremely hard water or excesses of certain ions, such as iron, can complicate the growing of plants in containers (and in gardens). If you live in such a region, contact your local botanical garden for suggestions on how to overcome these problems.

Variations in water quality can occur from season to season if your municipality draws water from streams or a reservoir where evaporation or flooding can change the concentration of salts. Water quality often gets commercial growers in trouble. It is one of the factors to suspect when plants don't grow as they should.

Finally, recycled potting soil contains residual nutrients from past feedings. Except for phosphorus, which leaches away slowly, these will usually leach out in drainage water within a month after you pot up your new plants.

Don't be put off by the numerous variables in feeding plants. I have included them for the benefit of inquisitive gardeners who like to understand why things work as they do. You don't have to be a chemist to grow plants; you don't have to know the difference between an ion and a molecule. With just a little practice and respect for recommended application rates, you can grow the best-looking container plants you have ever seen.

CHAPTER 8

Seeding, Planting, and Transplanting

Sowing seeds or transplanting plants in containers is sinfully easy. You don't have to till or dig and rake the soil as you do in a garden, and instead of getting down on your knees, you can lift the containers for convenient access. Still, as with gardening in the ground, there are a few matters that need attention before you plant.

Pick up a handful of potting soil or planter mix from the bag or bale and squeeze it. If it balls up, then springs back when you release the pressure, it has about the right moisture content. If it seems quite dry, pour a gallon at a time into a clean wheelbarrow or garbage can, spray it with water, mix, and continue until the entire batch is moist. Bone-dry potting soils will wet faster if you mix about a teaspoon of surfactant into each gallon of warm water and use the solution for wetting. Remember, though, that you want damp soil, not sopping wet soil. If there is too much moisture, the mixture will tend to pack down too densely

when you fill containers and tap them on a bench to settle the contents.

When the soil is properly damp, mix in the ingredients outlined in the chapters on planter mixes and fertilizers: perlite to lighten the mix, lime, fertilizers, and possibly an absorbent to increase water-holding capacity. The additives mingle more thoroughly and stay mingled when the soil is moist; in dry soil, the heavy particles tend to settle to the bottom.

Planting Seeds

If you find it wasteful to buy a packet of seeds of lettuce, spinach, green onions, or sweet alyssum for planting in a

[178]

container or two, save your leftover seeds for successive plantings. Fold over the top of the seed packets, seal them in a jar with a packet of desiccant from a can of ground coffee, and store them in the refrigerator. They should keep for at least a year.

You can grow vegetables or flowers from seeds by two methods: by starting early indoors and transplanting, or by direct-seeding where the plants are to remain. When you start indoors, sow the seeds according to directions in small flats or in shallow pots of seed-starting mix, eight to twelve weeks before the average spring frost-free date for your area. When you direct-seed vegetables or flowers in larger containers filled with planter mix, start two or three weeks ahead of the time recommended on the seed packet, and plan to shelter the container in a protected location.

Either way, scatter the seeds around the top of the container, perhaps two or three seeds to every square inch, then dress a little planting mix on top of them. The rule of thumb for planting is to cover seeds to three times their diameter. If you goof and cover them deeper than recommended, they will probably germinate anyway, because planter mixes don't form crusts or bake hard. Give the seeded containers a good sprinkling of water, but don't spray so vigorously that the seeds are dislodged and washed around. Use a fan-shaped rose sprinkler head on your hose, and keep the water at low pressure until the seedlings have emerged and put on some growth.

When you start seeds indoors, cover the seeded mix with clear plastic wrap or two or three layers of newspaper to keep it from drying out. Seeds germinate best at temperatures of 70° to 75°F. Even those that will sprout at much lower temperatures — spinach and cabbage, for example — will come up quickly with more heat. Look around your house for warm places to start seeds, such as the furnace room or on top of the water heater or refrigerator (the warmth extracted by the coils has to go somewhere!).

The most important step in starting plants from seeds is to watch the seeded containers like a hawk. Remove the covers as soon as the first seeds sprout; don't wait for all of them to come up. Move the container to a cooler area for growing the seedlings; 60° to 65°F is ideal. If you forget and leave the seeds in the warm sprouting area too long, they will grow long, spindly stems that will never develop normally. Seedlings (young plants grown from seeds) grow best where the air is cool and the sunlight is strong. If you don't have strong sunlight, lower fluorescent lights until they nearly touch the tops of the seedlings and leave them on sixteen to eighteen hours a day.

Watch for the disease called damping-off, which can kill seeds and seedlings. Caused by a fungus, it prevents seeds from germinating and causes seedlings to topple over. You can avoid it entirely by using sterile seed-starting mixes, watering judiciously, germinating seeds at warm temperatures, and giving seedlings plenty of light.

Starting seeds in containers outdoors after the weather has warmed up is even easier. By late spring, the sunlight has grown so strong that it can balance the warm to hot temperatures. Seedlings will grow strong and "thrifty," an old-fashioned word that describes short, sturdy, well-branched, dark green seedlings.

You can transplant seedlings to larger containers outdoors when they are still very small. Prick (pry and lift) the seedlings out of the seed-starting mix with an ice cream stick or a pencil. Handle seedlings by their leaves rather than by their stems, which can be crushed easily. Simply poke holes in the moist planter mix with your finger, insert the seedlings to about the same depth they were in the seedling flat, and pinch the soil gently around them. Water them carefully and set the container in the shade for a day or two to ease their adjustment.

Work rapidly when you are transplanting; tiny seedlings can dry out quickly. If you started more seedlings than you have room for, transplant a few at a time. Seedlings will hold for several weeks awaiting transplanting.

Starting with Plants

✤

Many gardeners prefer to buy a six-pack of young plants of vegetables or annual flowers rather than to start with seeds. Plants cost a bit more but are convenient. You don't even need a trowel for planting; just stick your fingers three or four inches deep into the planter mix and pull it back to make a hole the size of the plant's root ball.

However, before you put the plant into the hole, look at the root ball. If the outside is matted with roots, the plant is potbound and needs some help. Pull off and discard the mat of roots circling the bottom of the root ball and, using your fingers, gently split the root system halfway up from the bottom. This spreads the roots out, exposes root tips so they can grow, and loosens the compacted root ball. It sounds traumatic, but just try transplanting without it. Dig up a potbound plant after two weeks; you will find that the roots have continued to spiral round and round and are largely restricted to the root-ball area.

Transplanting larger plants to sizable freestanding containers, windowboxes, and hanging baskets requires an approach that you would figure out for yourself after one try. Begin by assembling, moistening, and modifying your planter mix. Tap the plant out of its pot by inverting the pot and tapping the rim against a bench or worktable while you support the root ball with your free hand. Some nurseries split metal containers with a special tool, so all you have to do is bend back the two sides. If the root ball falls apart when you tap out the plant, return the plant to the nursery or grow it in its pot for about a month to strengthen its root system.

Rub off any roots that are circling the outside of the root ball, and prune off the heavier ones. Lay the root ball on its side and rub or pull off the mat of roots at the bottom, so that new feeder roots will proliferate and grow into the surrounding planter mix. Measure the root ball from top to bottom. If it is too tall to fit into a shallow, wide container, carefully pull it apart at the bottom to spread out the root system. Measure it again, and if necessary add planter mix to the bottom of the container to elevate the plant. Position the plant so that the top of the root ball is an inch or two below the rim of the container. Finally, scoop up planter mix and fill in around the root ball. Bang the container down once or twice to settle the contents. Don't ram the mix around the roots with your hands; subsequent watering will settle it sufficiently. Leave a headspace of one to two inches to serve as a water reservoir.

When you are dividing choice perennials, ground covers, or thickety shrubs in your garden, think about planting the divisions in containers. Wash the soil off the roots, prune off frayed root tips, add enough mix to the container to bring the plant up to the proper position, spread out the roots, and fill in around them. Water the plant to settle the mix and set the containers in a shady spot for a few days. In the North, transplant perennials in the spring; fall transplanting works better south of Zone 6.

Transplants inevitably suffer a certain amount of shock, and don't send out many new roots for two or three weeks. They can use water in the interim, but not fertilizer. Hold off feeding them for about three weeks, then water the soil with a mild solution of high-phosphate starter fertilizer.

Planting in Special Containers

✤

Planting in windowboxes and large hanging baskets differs from setting a single plant into a container. Windowboxes and baskets are customarily stuffed tightly with blooming and foliage plants for instant effect. If you are working with a king-sized container and can reach it safely with a ladder, position and secure it first, then plant it.

(Even when filled with lightweight mixes, large planters can require four hands for lifting and securing.) Cover the bottom with enough planter mix to bring the tops of the root balls to within an inch of the rim. Prepare the plants, then cram them in closely. Pour in planter mix to fill the gaps and gently firm it down with your hands. Water, then add more mix to fill the settled spots. Leave a headspace; it is frustrating to have overfilled containers shed water like a duck's back.

One person can handle the transplanting of specimens growing in containers of up to ten-gallon size. However, a fifteen-gallon plant can weigh as much as 150 pounds, depending on the amount of sand or soil in the mix. Either draft a couple of strong young people as helpers or pay the nursery to do it. Most large nurseries will help you choose compatible plants for a large hanging basket or window-box, select the planter to hold them, plant it properly, deliver it to your home, and set it in place.

Terra-cotta strawberry jars are rather pesky to plant because of the configuration of the planting holes. Most gardeners fill in a little moist planter mix, thread a plant's top through from the inside, spread out the roots, and fill in with mix to the level of the next hole. This procedure works better than filling the strawberry jar first and trying to stuff the roots into the lipped holes.

In contrast, filling first and then planting works better for plant towers, for spherical baskets lined with sphagnum moss, and for hanging baskets. Professionals tap some of the soil off root systems to reduce their diameter, wrap them in a layer of moist long-fiber sphagnum moss, pry open a planting hole with their fingers, and stuff in the wrapped root ball.

Planting Bulbs

Plant daffodil and tulip bulbs thickly in containers: the idea is to produce a mass of color, not to leave room for the bulbs to multiply and naturalize. The best way is to fill the container to within four inches of the rim, level the mix, firm it down slightly with your hand, set the bulbs in so tightly that they almost touch, then cover with planter mix to within an inch of the rim. Leveling the "floor" assures equal planting depth for all the bulbs and is essential to having them all bloom at the same time.

Plant lily bulbs in threes when you use five-gallon containers and in groups of five in seven-gallon sizes. Follow the directions on the package for planting depths. Certain hybrids put out roots from the bottom of the bulb and can be planted at a three-inch depth.

Plant caladium corms in threes or fives in five- or seven-gallon containers too, but much shallower than lilies. Fill the container first. Position the corms, push them down gently to establish contact with the planter mix, and barely cover them with more mix. Plant miniature gladiolus corms in much the same fashion, but thickly, as you would space tulips.

You can "overplant" a container of tulip or daffodil bulbs with early-blooming annuals or perennials such as forget-me-nots, johnny-jump-ups, or sweet alyssum. The bulbs will push up through them, and you will have two layers of color. The total effect is better than with bulbs planted alone, but you should use flowers that bloom at the same time as the bulbs.

CHAPTER 9

Watering

There is more to watering plants in containers than hooking up the hose and giving them a drenching. Sensible watering is much like the seat-of-the-pants flying of old-time pilots: you react to the feel of the wind on your face, the heat on your back, the clouds in the sky, the season of the year, the size and age of the plant, and the empirical measures at hand. You probe the planter mix with a finger. You heft the smaller containers. You tap the side of terra-cotta containers and listen for a ring or a thud. You flip a leaf or two to see whether they are plump or limp. You look as closely at the new growth of the plant as a pilot would at the terrain of an emergency landing strip.

Knowing When to Water

☙

The first thing to test is the moisture content of the soil. You can't do it by looking at the surface. You need to probe deeply with a finger to test for moisture two or three inches beneath the surface. With terra-cotta or thin concrete pots, you can rap the side with a metal knife handle. A dry container will ring; a moist one will thud. The most accurate gauge of all is to lift smaller pots; if they are heavy, they contain plenty of water. Just looking closely at a plant will often tell you whether it is too dry. The secret is to apply water just before the plant shows symptoms of stress so plainly that it is already in trouble. If a plant can get by without watering, skip it and check it again at the end of the day. (If it ain't broke, don't fix it!)

The second thing to consider is the size and age of the plant. Young or recently transplanted plants can't use much water and are often planted in oversize containers to give them room to develop. They have a large reserve of water to tide them over. Medium-size to large plants, especially those growing lushly, can drink a container dry within six or eight hours on a dry day. However, old plants can fool you. It seems that they are always hollering for water; you would think they are using it at a great rate. But if you were to tap out the root ball, you would find it matted with girdling roots, many dead or devoid of feeder rootlets. Much of the soil will have been used up or oxidized and replaced by roots. What is left of the planter mix can't absorb much water, and roots may be clogging the drainage holes. Obviously, you can't tap out and repot a fully grown tomato plant living in a thirty-gallon container, but you can root-prune smaller potbound plants and then shift them to larger containers.

The season and the current weather also affect the need for watering. In cool or cloudy weather, plants transpire relatively little moisture from their leaves, and not much moisture is lost to evaporation from the surface of the soil. Rain may supply all the water your container plants need. But during warm, windy weather, evaporation and transpiration increase to keep the plant cool and to prevent it from wilting beyond the point of recovery. You may have to water twice daily on days that are too hot for yard work. Of course, plants can look pitiful by three o'clock and then shape up by seven or eight o'clock on their own, as water stress declines. It is when they don't recover that you had best start worrying; nurserymen call that condition terminal wilt.

Western gardeners who live with alkaline water have to water more often than their eastern counterparts. Plants can tolerate fairly high levels of salts in the water, but you must not allow the soil to dry out. Damage occurs when the soil becomes so dry and alkaline that exosmosis draws water out of plant roots. Salts that accumulate in the planter mix as water evaporates can kill roots. Gardeners in the West know to flush containers with heavy waterings every week or so to dissolve and drain away excess residues. Those fortunate enough to receive snowmelt have no such problems; alkalinity is highest where water is drawn from rivers or lakes, especially when water levels are low from overuse or summer evaporation.

Watering Methods

❦

I recommend attaching a water breaker or rose showerhead to the end of a hose for watering containers. Water breakers reduce the velocity of the stream of water and convert it into a broad, gentle flow. The most convenient and durable design is an aluminum wand two to four feet long, with the pressure reducer or perforated head on the end. You can reach both plants on the ground and those up in hanging baskets with ease. A simple little fan-shaped rose sprinkling head will also suffice, but it tends to blast the soil when the pressure is turned up. Keep the water breaker for container plants separate from the ones you use in the garden, to reduce the chance of infecting container soil mixes with nematodes or root-rot organisms from garden soil.

I know that many gardeners get by without a water breaker on the end of their hose. They reduce the flow and cup their hand over the end to break the force of the blast. This works pretty well in preventing the planter mix from being washed around, and the water doesn't dig deep holes in the root ball. But try it with a hanging basket and you will get cold water down your arm and body and into your shoes!

It is important to move the water breaker over the surface of the root ball to ensure that it is wet throughout. If you merely lay the head in one spot and let it run, you may wet a cone from top to bottom but leave some of the root ball dry. Every time you water, make sure that some runs out the bottom of the container; this shows not only that you have applied enough but that you have flushed residues out, just as a good rain would do.

If you notice that water is running down around the perimeter of the root ball and immediately sluicing out the drainage holes, it is time to add a surfactant to your water.

As explained in Chapter 6, these nontoxic soaplike compounds "make water wetter" by reducing the surface tension of droplets. Add about a teaspoon per gallon of water, mix it in, and pour the solution slowly onto the root ball until a little runs out the bottom. Some people recommend adding liquid dishwashing detergent, the kind you squeeze out of a bottle, to the water. This is a holdover from the days when Grandma swore by Octagon or Fels Naptha soap for watering rosebushes. The only way to be completely sure that a surfactant is safe for plants is to buy one that is formulated for that purpose and has been proven nontoxic. If you buy a year's supply at a time, a jug won't cost much more than an equivalent quantity of detergent.

After you water, not before, is the time for liquid feeding. Try to imagine every particle of planter mix in the root ball swollen with water and a fair amount of water clinging to each shred of peat moss or pine bark. Then imagine pouring a bucket of fertilizer solution or manure tea slowly over the top of the root ball. Much of the water in and around the particles will be displaced by the nutrient-laden solution pressing down from above. If you poured the same solution over a bone-dry root ball, perhaps already salty or alkaline with residues from previous feedings and from alkaline water, the particles wouldn't absorb water at all, or at the most only a small amount. The salts in the nutrient solution, combined with those already in the soil, might burn some sensitive feeder roots. Water before you feed!

If you are clever, you may be able to rig up an automatic watering system for your containers. This allows you to go away for a weekend or a week and not worry about your container plants. You can splice together a drip irrigation system using an inexpensive, flexible black or gray plastic tube for your main hose, small-diameter spaghetti tubes for delivery, weighted drop heads to hold the delivery tubes in place, an inexpensive timer, and a filter to take out grit. Use

a leather punch to make holes for the spaghetti tubes, and buy little grommetlike brass fittings that retain a tight link. If you move your containers around, plug holes in the main plastic tube with short, thick sheet-metal screws.

When you set up an automatic watering system or when you fall into a routine of watering only the surface of the root ball, remember that plants like an occasional bath to remove dust and to wash away insect eggs and pests such as spider mites. During the summer, load up your pump sprayer with water or a mild solution of insecticidal soap and give each plant a thorough shower from below. Reach in to the center of the plant with the uptilted spray head and walk around it to clean the undersides of all the leaves and the flower and leaf buds. Use enough pressure to make the leaves dance but not enough to blow them off or tatter their margins.

Finally, it's helpful to understand what happens when you flood the headspace of a container with water. The weight of the column of water drives oxygen and gases down and out of the drainage holes, although some may bubble up through the pond of water at the top. Then, as the excess water drains out of the holes in the bottom of the container, air spaces open up between the soil particles. The new air charges the soil with oxygen and invigorates the aerobic microorganisms that convert the compounds in fertilizers or manure tea to nutrients available to plants. As the soil on or near the surface dries, capillary action draws moisture from deep levels to replace it. This is why the assortment of particle sizes in your planter mix or potting soil is so important — why it can provide good drainage and oxygenation, yet not result in a too-dry mixture.

I liken manmade soils to bumblebees. In aerodynamic terms, bees shouldn't be able to fly. In technical terms, artificial soils shouldn't function as well as nature's own. But they can, and they do . . . if you water well and wisely.

CHAPTER 10

Winter Care

If you grow annual flowers or vegetables, you can skip this chapter, since all you need to do after the growing season ends is to dump them on the compost heap. Hardy perennials, bulbs, shrubs, trees, and, in the South and West, citrus and foliage plants and succulents are another matter. Wintering them over is tricky and sometimes risky. A lot depends on where you live. Moreover, cold weather affects not only plants but their containers, almost all of which can be destroyed by freezing and thawing. Terra-cotta and wood containers are the most vulnerable, but plastic pots can also shatter. Solid concrete, heavy fiberglass, and concrete-and-asbestos containers are the most durable.

If I lived in Zone 4 or 5, I would not attempt to keep any plants outdoors over the winter — although I know of at least one gardener in Chicago who has learned to maintain hardy perennials on her rooftop garden all year round. It is possible to move containers into a cool but not freezing cellar or garage for the winter and thus keep deciduous plants in a dormant condition until the following spring.

They need very little water; thorough watering once a month will leach out accumulating salts and prevent roots and top tissues from desiccating. It is also possible to move tender and tropical plants in containers to a cool sunporch, where they receive plenty of light but are not in danger of freezing; they may lose their leaves, but they winter over very well. Yet I wouldn't want to have to walk around and over container plants for five or six months of the year. To me, annual flowers, vegetables, and herbs are more practical and nearly as satisfactory. One of the few exceptions I would make is for tender fruit trees such as figs; they are well worth the trouble of winter protection.

Zone 6 is a tough climate zone. Most years you can grow a few species with no winter protection — junipers, hardy deciduous shrubs, miniature roses, and such. Then along comes a fierce winter that will wipe out everything, unless you have taken steps to minimize the effects of frigid temperatures. Generally, the larger the container is, the better chance your plant has of surviving.

Consider what happens to a containerized plant in extremely cold weather. The root ball, exposed to cold air on all sides and perhaps underneath, plunges to much lower temperatures than soil in the garden. Conversely, on warm days its temperature zooms higher than the temperature of garden soil. Freezing and thawing can cause the plant to lift up or heave out of the soil, which exposes and breaks its roots. Winters are often dry, with no rain or snow for weeks on end. Temperatures within the root ball may exceed the 40° minimum required for root growth, but without sufficient water the plant suffers, particularly on windy days.

A great deal of experimentation is underway in Zone 6 and the northern half of Zone 7 to find ways to reduce winter damage. Simply setting containers on garden soil rather than on pavement or wood helps a little, but the bottom of the pot serves as a barrier that reduces heat transmission from the soil.

The best approach is to insulate your containers at the time of planting. Line square or rectangular containers with sheets of Styrofoam, and pack foam plastic nuggets or long-fiber, ropy sphagnum moss underneath and around the root ball in cylindrical containers. Insulating against winter damage also minimizes root damage from intense summer sun. (Black containers can absorb so much heat that roots on the "afternoon side" can be destroyed.)

If you use foam plastic sheets, cut the side pieces so they will not protrude above the soil. Foam nuggets tend to float out or blow away, so when you position the root ball, set it one and a half to two inches lower than you ordinarily would and mulch the top with long-fiber sphagnum moss or hardwood bark. Either should hold the nuggets in place. Setting your plant, container and all, inside a larger container and filling the space with insulation helps somewhat, but isn't as effective as surrounding the root ball itself with insulation.

If you want to protect container plants that were not insulated at planting time, start by setting them on the ground. To provide additional protection, pull pine needles or hay, pine-bark nuggets, or hardwood mulch around them. Banking soil around the containers serves the same purpose, but soil tends to wash away or settle.

If these measures fail to protect your plants fully, consider tapping them out of their containers and hilling up around them with garden soil. Store the empty containers in a dry place and repot the plants in early spring, after the intensely cold weather.

Occasional severe winters in Zone 7 can give semihardy evergreen container plants a rough time. During the mid-1980s, a below-zero spell that lasted for nearly a week killed many container plants. When temperatures below about 20°F are forecast, move your containers to a garage or toolshed and wrap them in old blankets. If you can use a space heater to keep the air temperature above freezing, you will avoid the damage to foliage that wrapping and unwrapping plants with blankets can cause. Overnight temperatures in the thirties or the upper twenties should not harm semihardy or hardy plants.

You should shake conifers, such as junipers, after a heavy snowfall or ice storm to prevent the accumulated weight from breaking limbs. Pines in containers will bend over beneath a snow load but will straighten up when the snow is shaken off or melts.

In Zone 6 and south, alternate freezing and thawing of the foliage and tender bark of evergreens causes more problems than the destructive freezing of root balls. You can best avoid this by moving container plants to the north or east side of your house, where they will be in the shade for much of the day. You can spray broad-leaved evergreen plants in fixed containers such as planter boxes with an antitranspirant to reduce winter foliage burn on windy days. To prevent bark damage, wrap the plant with tree tape, the kind used to protect trunks of young fruit trees from sun damage. You can spray the lower trunks with flat white latex, but most gardeners object to the effect.

Zones 8, 9, and 10 present a different set of challenges for winter care. Except during a few midwinter weeks in upper Zone 8, root-ball temperatures average higher than 40°F. Thus, root and top growth continues during the winter — albeit at a reduced rate, since soil temperatures are much lower than during the summer — and there is microbiological activity in the container soil, although it too is reduced. The rate of conversion of ammoniac nitrogen to the nitrate form available to plants slows, and plants take on a yellowish appearance. With less frequent watering, salts tend to build up in the root ball, and the pH of the soil rises. Deficiencies of iron and zinc are apt to occur, because these nutrients are less available to plants at higher pH levels. Winter rainfall is fairly heavy in some areas of the South and West, and leads to leaching of plant nutrients, particularly nitrogen and potassium.

Because of these factors, the major consideration in winter care for container plants in the Deep South and warm West is maintaining good foliage color with applications of fertilizer and, if needed, micronutrients such as iron and zinc. Foliar feeding will "green up" the foliage of broadleaved evergreens and citrus plants faster than applications of dry plant food. For winter feeding, be sure the nitrogen in your fertilizer is mostly in the nitrate form, except for acid-loving plants such as blueberries, azaleas, pieris, and mountain laurels. Some fertilizers are especially formulated for these plants; they contain nitrogen in the ammoniac form and leave a mildly acid residue.

In areas where winters are rainy and rather warm, container plants can suffer from soggy bottoms, often caused by the settling of the growing medium, which in turn is caused by oxidation of organic particles, utilization by plants, or gravitation of fine particles to the bottom layers. Technically, the condition is caused by a "perched" water table, which means that water fails to drain completely from the bottom layers of the root ball. Soggy bottoms can also occur in terribly potbound plants that have formed a mat of girdling roots at the bottom of the container. These can nearly close off drainage holes and impede proper runthrough of excess water.

I realize that inspecting the root balls of plants in large containers is not always an easy job, but you should do it yearly, when going into the winter. Run a long knife between the container sides and the soil. Lay the container on its side and slide the plant out, root ball and all. Inspect the root ball and cut and remove any girdling roots. If the plant is not potbound, put it back in the same container. If it is, scratch the surface of the root ball to force root tips to proliferate, then shift the plant to the next largest container and fill in around it with new planter mix.

If you are concerned about exposing container plants to possible winter injury or loss, visit a nearby botanical garden or a large, full-service nursery and ask the employees about their experience with winter survival of plants. More than anyone else, they have firsthand experience, and can help you select hardy cultivars and durable containers. Their advice will help you feel secure about your container plants during the coldest weather of the year.

CHAPTER 11

Insects and Diseases

Although plants grown in containers are less prone to plagues than those grown in the garden, you won't get off scot-free — not always. Insects and diseases have always been with us and always will be, so you might as well be philosophical about them. Fortunately, much more is now known about controlling these problems without toxic chemicals than was known just a few years ago, and gardeners can often get good results with a combination of organic controls instead of nuking a pest or disease with a broad-spectrum chemical.

A central precept of organic gardening is how to tell the good guys of the insect world from the bad guys, and how to tell disease symptoms from nutrient deficiencies and weather stresses. Some states publish bulletins about controlling plant problems organically, whereas others still recommend only the chemicals found on garden-center shelves. Agricultural scientists in warmer climates, especially where the humidity is high, tend to favor chemical controls, because insect and disease problems tend to be more severe in their areas.

Insects

METHODS OF CONTROL
■ ■ ■

Gardeners who are just learning how to control insects the organic way tend to rely on the natural insecticides called botanicals, the cultured microorganisms called biologicals, and insecticidal soaps. Botanicals include pyrethrum and its extract, pyrethrin, and rotenone, sabadilla, and ryania. Although naturally occurring substances or extracts, these are poisons and must not be applied carelessly. Biologicals include various strains of bacilli and microsporidia that are effective against certain types of insect larvae and juveniles. Insecticidal soaps contain a complex of potassium salts of fatty acids, highly refined soaps that either repel insects or cut through their chitin and cause them to dry out.

A new and totally safe form of insect control is floating row covers, which keep insects completely away from plants. They make container plants look like furniture covered for storage, but with a little study you can learn to cover susceptible plants only during the period when adult flies or moths are laying eggs.

Advanced organic gardeners release predaceous insects such as ladybugs, praying mantises, *Trichogramma* and *Encarsia* wasps, and predatory mites to control pests without using botanicals or biologicals. Often they succeed, and their successes will become more numerous as scientists learn how to cultivate additional beneficial insects.

Taking the time to look closely at insects before deciding what to do about them makes sense. Predatory insects such as lacewings and assassin and ambush bugs usually feed on injurious insects. If you see them at work, hold off on spraying or dusting and let them do their job. However, if the concentration of harmful insects is great enough to worry you, wait until sundown, when bees and most of the predators have retired, to spray or dust.

Insect species are so numerous and vary so much from climate to climate that identification can be difficult. Bulletins from your county Cooperative Extension Service deal with the pests that trouble agricultural and garden crops in your locale, and, coupled with a color book on identifying insects, may be sufficient. I've had a copy of the late Dr. Cynthia Westcott's *The Gardener's Bug Book* in my library for nearly twenty years; it is my ultimate reference. The insecticides listed in it have changed, but the bugs haven't.

If insects trouble your container plants, you can eradicate them without upsetting the ecology of your entire yard. Container plants are usually relatively small, few in number, and elevated; with a hand sprayer, you can reach all surfaces of leaves to apply biological or botanical controls or simply blast insects off with clear water or insecticidal soap. Small trigger-operated or pump-action hand sprayers are inexpensive and easy to load and clean. Hand-cranked dusters make it easy to apply botanical dusts, but they are less efficient than sprays.

Plants grown in containers always get closer attention than those grown in the garden, and they get it more frequently. It is easy to monitor them for discolored, disfigured, or chewed foliage. Discolored foliage can be caused by nutrient shortages, but with a little practice you can quickly distinguish starved leaves from those sucked dry by insects.

SUCKING INSECTS

■ ■ ■

Sucking or rasping insects come in five major classes: whiteflies, spider mites, aphids, thrips, and leafhoppers.

Whiteflies are the scourge of tomato and marigold plants especially, and of ornamentals with large, felty leaves. Brush against an infested plant and a cloud of small white flies will flutter up your nose and cling to your clothes. They breed like . . . well, flies. It seems that every two or three days a new hatch emerges from eggs laid on the underside of leaves. Actually, the egg-to-adult life cycle of whiteflies takes about thirty to forty days, depending on temperature. However, generations overlap and produce new individuals every few days.

Whiteflies not only weaken and stunt plants by sucking their juices; they can also carry plant disease organisms in their systems and inject them when feeding. You can control them, but once you have knocked them out you have to remain watchful, because more can fly over from a neighbor's plants. The insecticidal soaps are about as effective as any of the synthetics, but be sure to spray with them every two or three days until most of the eggs have hatched and you have killed the adults. Whiteflies congregate on the undersides of leaves, so you must spray from underneath to get at them. The *Encarsia* wasp feeds on whiteflies but is effective only when confined in greenhouses.

You aren't aware of **spider mites** until you begin to see plants with dusty-looking, speckled, and flecked leaves. When you turn the leaves over, you might see a few tiny eight-legged mites crawling around on the undersides, but most people need a 10-power glass to see them clearly. More probably you will see webby strands and gritty deposits of excreta. If you don't control spider mites quickly, they will spread over the entire plant, weaken or kill it, then move on to others. They can infest almost all species of plants but are especially bad on snap beans, tomatoes, strawberries, junipers, azaleas, citrus plants, and plants with hairy undersides to their leaves.

Spider mite populations seem to explode in hot, dry weather. Under optimum conditions and at 70°F, one female could breed a population of 12,000 mites in one month, assuming no mortality along the way. At a constant temperature of 80° for a month, that female could expand to 13,000,000 mites!

The general run of chemical insecticides — Malathion and the synthetic pyrethroids, for example — do little to control spider mites, perhaps because these little animals can develop resistance to them. Organic gardeners spray mite-infested plants with insecticidal soap, homemade mixtures of garlic and hot-pepper juice, or sharp, fine jets of water, or they dust them with pyrethrum, which is made from the dried petals of painted daisies.

Aphids, or plant lice, are most troublesome in rather cool, moist weather. They don't attract attention as white-flies and spider mites do, and can feed and multiply for some time until you happen to notice them clinging by the dozens to tender stems and emerging buds. How they reproduce! They reach sexual maturity in about ten days and may give birth to as many as six live young — all females — per hour.

Aphids have swollen abdomens and can be whitish, green, or brown. Some can fly; most don't. They are easier to control than either whiteflies or spider mites, but more often carry and inject plants with disease organisms, such as the viruses that cause mosaic and the mycoplasma responsible for aster yellows. Roses, chrysanthemums, and other flowers as well as vegetables, shrubs, and fruit trees are susceptible to aphid damage. Organic gardeners watch for "hot spots" of aphid outbreaks and restrict their spraying accordingly, using the same controls as for spider mites. Certain manufacturers of botanical controls make concentrated blends of rotenone and pyrethrin to control aphids and other soft-bodied insects.

A fourth kind of insect, **thrips**, can cause problems too. These tiny creatures crawl inside buds and distort their growth, and stipple petals and foliage with their rasping mouthparts. They can prevent tomato blossoms from fruiting or create roughness on the blossom end of the fruit. You may have seen thrip damage on daisylike flowers: it shows as lopsided blossoms on which the petals are missing or stunted on one side. One species, the western flower thrip, can transmit the tomato spotted wilt virus, a devastating disease, to peppers, Irish potatoes, and many ornamentals as well as tomatoes.

If you grow chrysanthemums, roses, or dahlias, you might have to schedule preventive spray programs to keep thrips from entering and spoiling flower buds. They can also reduce fruit tree blooms and spoil the set on nut trees. Thrips are not as hard to control as whiteflies or spider mites, but you must not wait to spray until you see damaged flowers or fruiting buds. You may have to add wettable powdered rotenone to insecticidal soap to control these insects.

Last but not least among the tiny sucking insects are the many kinds of **leafhoppers**. Their wings are either raised in the center like a roof or humped on one end like a buffalo. Leafhoppers come in many colors; some are striped. Most species have large eyes. They feed by gouging trenches in leaf tissue and lapping up sap. I have had success in controlling them with insecticidal soap at near maximum application rates, but I have achieved equal control at lower rates by mixing pyrethrin with the soap.

BUGS

In addition to the little suckers there are a bunch of big suckers, or true bugs — not moths, flies, mites, or beetles, but fast-moving bugs that suck plant juices through tubular bills. True bugs are flattened-looking; many are shaped like shields. Some are not much larger than aphids, but they scuttle or fly around so actively that you'll never confuse the two. The most important pests among the true bugs are **harlequin bugs, squash bugs, stinkbugs, four-lined plant bugs, leaf-footed bugs, lace bugs, tarnished plant bugs,** and **chinch bugs.** These true bugs can cause a lot of damage in a short time because they multiply rapidly. Make an effort to distinguish them from beneficial true bugs, such as ambush and assassin bugs, big-eyed bugs, and damsel bugs.

We gardeners have only a few controls for these insects. Rotenone dust or a combination rotenone-and-pyrethrin spray does a pretty good job. However, some of the true bugs, such as squash bugs, green stinkbugs, and harlequin bugs, are partially protected by a leathery exoskeleton and are difficult to kill. You may have to switch to a stronger botanical control, sabadilla, also sold under the brand name Red Devil.

BEETLES

Beetle species make up about 40 percent of all insects, and include the specialized types known as snout beetles (curculios or weevils) and the adult stage of some borers. You can recognize beetles by their wing sheaths, which are divided down the middle from stem to stern. Many beneficial insects are ground beetles, but you will rarely see them around container plants.

Among the most troublesome beetles on popular container plants are the many species of flea beetles, Japanese beetles, cucumber beetles, Colorado potato beetles, rose chafers, plum curculios, and white-fringed beetles. Rotenone dust or a rotenone-and-pyrethrin spray is the most effective short-lived insecticide for these pests. Really tough customers such as cucumber or asparagus beetles may call for sabadilla or another botanical, ryania.

The **flea beetles** got their name because of their habit of jumping when disturbed. They range from the size of a pinhead to that of a sesame seed and cause the most damage during the early stages of growth of seedlings. If uncontrolled, they can riddle leaves with small shot holes, causing them to turn brown. Eggplant and tomato seedlings and potato shoots are especially attractive to flea beetles. Rotenone is the best control.

Gardeners in the Midwest, Southwest, and West have yet to experience the frustration of coping with **Japanese beetles.** All over the East, especially in the middle section, these rather small, shiny, coppery-green and black beetles wing in to devour the flowers and foliage of many garden plants. Early summer is their arrival time; just when depends on how early the season is. On a farm or a large lot you can hang beetle traps some distance upwind from your garden and trap them as they fly in, but traps within your garden merely attract your neighbor's pests to feed on your flowers. If you have just a few container plants, hand-pick the beetles daily and drop them into a can of gasoline or solvent. They wiggle furiously but don't bite or sting. Japanese beetles hang around for four to six weeks, then disappear.

A biological control for Japanese beetles, milky spore disease, has been available for many years. However, because the beetles fly, success with using it depends on the treatment of rather large areas, which in turn depends on unanimous cooperation among neighbors. Holdouts can negate the effects of the program, and not everyone understands the benefits of using specific biological controls.

Cucumber beetles, which are either spotted or striped, feed on the roots, foliage, and flowers of many garden species in their larval and adult stages. Their most serious effect is the transmittal of bacterial wilt to melons and of cucumber mosaic virus, which apparently has developed the ability to infect flower and other vegetable species. Sabadilla dust is recommended as a control, but floating row covers are more effective.

Colorado potato beetles are pests not only on potatoes but on related solanaceous plant species, such as eggplants, tomatoes, peppers, ground cherries, tomatillos, nicotianas, and petunias. The medium-sized adult beetles are yellow and turtle-backed, with stripes and spots. The hump-backed, fat, orange-red larvae also destroy foliage. Hand-picking works well; some will do a quick free fall if you shake the foliage, but you can capture them the following day. Recently, a specific biological control has been perfected for these beetles; it is harmless to humans, pets, and beneficial insects.

Rose chafers are elongated tan beetles with brown heads and long legs. They feed on many species of ornamentals and on fruit trees and grapes. They are usually too numerous to hand-pick, so spray or dust with sabadilla to control them.

Plum curculios are one variety of the many **weevils** or **snout beetles** that destroy fruits, nuts, and flowers. They lay eggs that hatch into burrowing larvae. Damage from these pests can be confused with that from the borers that hatch from moth eggs and tunnel into fruit. Protective dusts of rotenone or sabadilla are the recommended protection; your Cooperative Extension Service can supply you with a schedule for application.

Gardeners in the Southeast and lower Midwest rue the day when **white-fringed beetles** were accidentally introduced. These medium-sized, brownish-gray beetles have short snouts and distinctive white stripes down their sides. Most of the damage is caused by their larvae, which feed on the roots of many species of ornamental or food plants. Because it is easy to mistake the damage for the sudden onset of root diseases, probe around, and if you see tiny larvae on or in the roots of your container plants, drench them with rotenone. Repeat this procedure a week later.

OTHER INSECT PESTS

Plants with thick stems or leaves or fleshy fruits can be attacked by **borers** and **grubs**, which are among the most frustrating of pests because you can't get at them without further injuring the plant. Furthermore, you are not likely to see the adults which lay the eggs that hatch into borers or grubs. Complicating the picture is the fact that immature moths, flies, and beetles, and in some cases adult beetles, will also bore. Sometimes you can tell that borers are at work because you can see their excreta or "frass," a word that I believe was invented by entomologists to avoid offending sensibilities. At other times you can't locate an entry hole but you know a borer is in a stem because it is wilting. In the Southeast, when we are pruning roses, we have to dab each cut with asphaltum or white paint to keep borers from entering through the wound.

Borers are most troublesome when plants are under stress from transplanting or drought. Careful probing with a sharp knife may disclose them. Clean out the area and either paint it or apply a commercial wound paint. If your plants are afflicted with the **squash vine borer**, slit the affected stem, fish out the larva, mound soil over the wounded part, and hope that the vine will strike roots and recover. Spraying a plant with an insecticide is pointless; the active ingredient won't penetrate and kill the pest. However, spraying a woody plant with an antidessicant when you are transplanting it seems to repel these creatures.

Among the most bothersome borers affecting container plants are the **peach tree borer**; the **lilac borer**; **birch, pine**, and **dogwood borers**; **twig girdlers**; the squash vine borer; and **berry cane, rhododendron**, and **iris borers**. It would seem that a beetle grub or moth or fly larva has evolved to attack almost every plant species. Your best defense is to keep plants well fed and watered. It doesn't do any good to spray or dust after the damage is detected; only preventive applications are effective.

Many larvae of moths, flies, and butterflies, including caterpillars, fruitworms, and pickleworms, don't bore into stems. Rather, they devour foliage and flowers, or burrow into melons or other fruit and cause them to spoil. The most notorious is the Medfly or **Mediterranean fruit fly**, which appears periodically in warm climates. Federal and state authorities pounce on outbreaks of this pest, which is considered dangerous enough to justify quarantines.

From a home garden standpoint, the larvae of the **imported cabbageworm** are probably the most serious and widespread pests. These green worms infest all cabbage family members — the cole crops. Yet the damage from cabbageworms pales by comparison with that from an invasion of **armyworms**. Hordes of these greenish-brown, striped caterpillars can march into gardens and strip many kinds of flowers and vegetables. Fortunately, these larvae, and most others, can be controlled with sprays of *Bacillus thuringiensis*, which is sold under many brand names. This nontoxic biological control takes a few days to kill worms after they ingest it, but it is thorough.

When you begin to recognize friends and foes, you will be able to identify certain caterpillars as the larvae of beautiful butterflies. For example, the larvae of monarch butterflies prefer plants of the milkweed family — butterfly weed and such. Larvae of the swallowtails prefer plants belonging to the parsley family — dill, carrots, fennel, and Queen Anne's lace. These larvae don't eat much. Leave them alone to grow into butterflies; you'll feel better about yourself if you don't pluck them off and stomp on them.

Among the flies whose larvae can trouble container plants are **carrot rust flies, leaf miners,** and **cherry fruit flies.** These all tunnel and can't be reached with sprays or dusts, so you'll have to use preventive spray programs or floating row covers to repel or exclude the adult flies. By and large, there are more beneficial than harmful flies, so I prefer floating row covers to poisons, even to the relatively safe botanicals.

Miscellaneous pests such as scales, spittlebugs, mealybugs, earwigs, slugs, and snails can bother container plants. **Scales** and **mealybugs** have protective coatings, so ordinary sprays and dusts aren't very effective. However, when you mix a small amount of surfactant with an insecticide and apply it when scales are crawling, it will coat these insects and kill them. A biological control — a predatory insect named *Cryptolaemus* — will fight mealybugs. Other beneficial insects are, if you will excuse the expression, waiting in the wings, pending the completion of tests of their efficiency and refinement of mass-production techniques.

Earwigs are fearsome-looking, night-feeding insects with rear appendages that resemble crab claws or forceps. They eat regular holes in leaves and petals with their mandibles, not with their rear appendages. You rarely see earwigs unless you go out at night and shine a flashlight on plants. They can be killed with rotenone.

Slugs and **snails** are also night feeders but leave more irregular holes, along with slime trails. They can be controlled with bait made of metaldehyde, a synthetic organic chemical that is unacceptable to organic gardeners. I use such bait, but not in a way that could injure children or pets or poison the soil. I put a tablespoon in a partially flattened frozen juice can and moisten it. Slugs and snails crawl in, partake, and expire. I have yet to use the organic control that the beer barons love — sinking shallow pans of beer flush with the soil surface to attract and drown the pesky mollusks.

Several ecology-minded companies now offer relatively or completely safe insecticides and insect repellents by mail. Some of these products are also sold through seed catalogues. For a directory of companies that specialize in botanical and biological controls, I refer you to Barbara Barton's excellent sourcebook, *Gardening by Mail*.

Diseases

When it comes to plant diseases, you see the symptoms rather than the organisms that cause them — bacteria, fungi, viruses, mycoplasmas, or nematodes. Actually, container plants suffer far fewer diseases than garden-grown plants. Plants grown in artificial soil are rarely affected by root diseases, and planter mixes are seldom contaminated with spores that can splash onto foliage and cause disease. Foliage diseases are less prevalent anyway because the plants are not crammed close together and are usually placed where their leaves can dry quickly. Nevertheless, you do need to know how to recognize the symptoms of the major classes of diseases, what (if any) controls to apply, and how.

When I attempt to diagnose a disease by symptoms, I look at the affected part of the plant. Foliage diseases are the easiest to see. They show up as spots, blotches, patchy gray or necrotic areas, or discolored leaves. Stems, fruits, and flowers can also be affected. Root diseases, which can be either localized or systemic, spread through the entire plant via its circulatory or vascular system, and often cause wilting, stunted growth, or yellowing foliage in addition to rotting roots. If you notice any of these symptoms among your container plants and are not sure how to proceed, contact your local Cooperative Extension Service, which will diagnose leaves, stems, or other plant parts at its Plant Problem Clinic or send a Master Gardener to your home to make an on-site diagnosis.

FUNGAL DISEASES

These diseases, caused by many different species and subspecies of fungi, are the most common and often affect foliage and roots. They are transmitted by all kinds of specialized spores or reproductive bodies, which can be carried to plants on the wind, in water, in splashed soil, by your hands, and by dirt-encrusted garden tools. The spores can live in the soil, in residues of previous crops, on and around weeds, in improperly composted organic waste, in manure . . . and can persist for years.

When you grow ornamentals or food crops in containers, the fungal diseases you may see include **downy** and **powdery mildew, anthracnose, early blight,** various **leaf spots, damping-off, fusarium root rot, gray mold** or botrytis, **rust,** certain **cankers, cabbage yellows** and **cabbage blackleg,** and **brown rot** and **scab** of peaches. No fungicides other than sulfur, lime-sulfur, and Bordeaux mix are acceptable to most organic gardeners. Your best bet is to reduce the possibility of infection by keeping water off foliage, making sure that your container soils drain well, and treating infected areas with sulfur dust.

One condition that can be diagnosed as a fungal disease is a moldy black coating on leaves of citruses and other ornamentals. Known as honeydew, it is actually caused by saprophytic organisms that grow in the honeydew secreted by aphids and other feeding insects. It is harmless but unattractive, and can usually be washed off with a sharp jet of water laced with a surfactant.

BACTERIAL DISEASES

Diseases caused by bacteria are among the most severe and can cause leaf spots, necrosis of foliage, blights, galls, slime, and occasionally wilts. Bacteria reproduce by splitting, and reproduction can proceed rapidly when conditions are right. They can live in host plants, within or on seeds or insects, in plant refuse, and in the soil, and can be carried, or vectored, to plants by water or by soil carried on tools or boots or splashed up by rain. One of the reasons that gardeners are cautioned not to pick beans when the foliage is wet is that bean blight can be vectored throughout a row by the moisture on the gardener's hands.

Garden seed companies are very careful not to import seeds from areas where seed-borne bacteria are endemic. You can buy chemical treatments to kill fungi on the seed coat, but it is virtually impossible to kill bacteria within the seed without ruining its germination. (There are no organically acceptable treatments to control fungal spores on seeds other than washing the seeds with strong soap, rinsing them, and drying them before planting.)

Among the bacterial diseases you may encounter on container-grown plants are crown gall, fireblight on pyracantha and pears, bacterial wilt on melons and cucumbers, and rust on beans, roses, and hollyhocks. Most bacterial diseases are systemic and difficult to control.

Crown gall, which affects fruit trees, is extremely hard to eradicate and may require you to get rid of the infected plant. To restrict **fireblight**, prune off infected twigs and branches or plant resistant varieties of pears. Dip your shears in alcohol after each cut. You can completely avoid **bacterial wilt** of melons and cucumbers by putting down floating row covers early in the season and leaving them in place until the weather becomes so hot that you must remove them. Control **rusts** with sulfur dust, but be careful not to apply it during hot weather. In summary, sprays and dusts control only the few bacterial diseases that are manifested as minor leaf spots and rust pustules.

VIRAL AND OTHER DISEASES

Viral diseases are caused by very small organisms that can pass through most filters, and are vectored by feeding insects. The most easily recognizable symptom is mottled, distorted leaves, called *mosaic*. Symptoms such as streaking, spotting, and yellowing and curling of leaves are common, and the usual total effect is a profound stunting and discoloration of the plant, slowed growth, and cessation of flowering or fruiting.

Although most virus-caused plant diseases are specific to one kind of plant, some, such as **cucumber** and **tobacco mosaic virus** and **tomato spotted wilt virus**, can infect a wide cross section of species. You should not smoke while handling your plants; tobacco mosaic virus can be carried in cigarette tobacco and vectored to container plants by your hands. One of the most serious viral diseases to emerge in recent years was the variety of **yellows disease** that killed entire avenues and groves of coconut palms in Florida, Mexico, and Central America.

With the viral diseases, strive to control the vectoring insects rather than the disease itself, as plants rarely recover once they have been infected. Floating row covers or preventive sprays can be effective. Pull out infected plants and dispose of them in the garbage, not on the compost heap, before the disease spreads. Remember that your hands can spread viral diseases from one plant to another, so always wash your hands after disposing of unhealthy plants. Don't buy any plants that appear less than 100 percent healthy, and as a rule, set aside purchased or gift plants for a week or so before planting and watch them closely for disease symptoms and vectoring insects.

Not much has been published in gardening books about the organisms called **mycoplasmas**. Until fairly recent years they were classed with the viruses, but now, since the disease called **aster yellows** has mutated and jumped to several species besides asters, including marigolds and petunias, scientists recognize mycoplasmas as distinct organisms. They are carried in the systems of feeding insects. Within a matter of days after infection, plants begin to turn light green, then cream or white, and they soon die. It is best to pull out infected plants as soon as the symptoms show, to limit the spread of the disease.

Nematodes are little multicelled organisms that are almost, but not quite, visible to the naked eye. Plants affected by them simply decline and die. Generally, nematodes are most troublesome in sandy soil and in warm climates. If you garden where they are prevalent, think twice before adding unsterilized garden soil or sand to otherwise pest-free planter mixes.

It's important to remember that this long list of insect and disease problems is a worst-case scenario. You will probably enjoy a lifetime of gardening in containers and not encounter more than one or two. Yet when the time comes that you do find them, if you have this information at hand, you won't think the sky is falling. To paraphrase an old Irish benediction, "May you have long departed this earth before the insects and diseases find your garden!"

Regional Plant Lists

I asked horticulturists at major public gardens, nurseries, and gardening magazines around the country to list some of their favorite container plants. These professionals not only propagate and grow plants but have a good eye for pleasing combinations of colors and textures.

Some of the plants listed will not be available at local nurseries and must be ordered from specialists. Barbara Barton's book *Gardening by Mail* lists mail-order sources of specialty plants. A few of the species are so esoteric that you may have to contact the public garden, nursery, or magazine to find a source.

This information has never before been published. In this appendix you will find so many good suggestions for plants in containers that you may run out of years in which to try them all. I've arranged the responses by geographical regions and have paraphrased for the sake of brevity.

NORTHEAST

Roger Swain
Science editor, *Horticulture,* Boston

Here in New England it is difficult to overwinter any plant in a container outdoors. Some woody species will survive, such as those in the venerable collection of bonsai at the Arnold Arboretum in Boston, but these have to be tapped out periodically and have their girdling roots pruned. My favorite container plants are those that are grown for one season only and then are discarded. These include not only annuals but quick-blooming perennials, houseplants, and tropicals, combined to personal preference. One-season plants are practical here; we need these islands of living color in the urban sea of concrete sidewalks and asphalt streets.

Dave Murbach
Director of horticulture, Rockefeller Management Corporation, New York City

Our gardens receive so much urban warmth that we can grow such plants as 'Newport Blue' boxwood (*Taxus densiformis*) and two junipers, 'Andorra' and *J. procumbens* 'Nana', for winter foliage. One of our most satisfactory displays had the theme "Texas Flora" and included southwestern yuccas and *Salvia greggii*. A plant we've come to rely on for fall color is *Helianthus salicifolius*. We use lots of the newer cultivars of daylilies, and *Euonymus alata* 'Compacta' for our roof gardens.

Leonard Besser
Curator, Staten Island Botanical Garden, New York

We like to use combinations of plants, such as geraniums with variegated ivy or vinca vine, or marigold 'Yellow Boy' with *Salvia farinacea* 'Victoria'. Visitors also like our hanging baskets of nasturtiums and Boston ferns. These plants are especially useful when we put together containers of foliage and flowering plants for special functions.

cabbage or kale for fall color. People especially seem to like the combination of *Caladium* 'Aaron' with *Impatiens* 'Blitz Violet' in partial shade.

Helmut Jaehnigan
Horticulturist, Behnke Nurseries, Beltsville, Maryland

For year-round plants in our cold-winter climate, we must use those that can withstand low soil temperatures. Among the most beautiful small trees for containers are the dwarf Japanese maples. The lace-leaf types do especially well here if grown in large-enough planters; they make attractive plants all year.

Dwarf flowering shrubs grow well in our containers. The miniature roses, miniflora roses, the new shrub rose 'Bonica', and most of the Meidiland roses winter over beautifully in containers of adequate size.

Many of the conifers are hardy for us. We use Alberta spruce, bird's-nest spruce, *mugo* pine, Japanese black pine, *Pinus flexilis* 'Glauca', *Pinus parviflora*, and *Pinus heldreichii* in containers. The junipers are quite hardy: the upright *J. chinensis* cultivars 'Torulosa', 'Robusta Green', and 'Wintergreen' combine well with the low creepers, such as *J. chinensis* var. *procumbens* 'Nana', 'Blue Pacific', 'San Jose', and 'Blue Rug'. 'Blue Pacific' is also good for trailing down the sides of a large container such as a half whiskey barrel.

Among the perennials, we have found that most sedum varieties, rudbeckia, hosta, lythrum, coreopsis, and the ornamental grasses are quite hardy in containers.

MIDDLE ATLANTIC STATES

⚜

Alan Thompson
Gardener, Brookside Gardens, Wheaton, Maryland

Some container plant combinations that have been well received by our public are *Asparagus densiflorus* 'Myers' with *Verbena* 'Border Blaze', bicolor crotons with *Lantana* 'Confetti', and hardy red, white, or yellow cushion chrysanthemums with ornamental

SOUTH AND SOUTHEAST

⚜

Carol Griffith
Horticulturist, Dixon Gallery and Gardens, Memphis

Some of our favorites are the 'Cocktail' series of wax begonias; the 'Universal' hybrid pansies — 'True Blue', 'Deep Yellow', 'Beaconsfield', 'Springtime', and 'Yellow Marble'; 'Mrs. Clibran' and 'Blue Stone' varieties of *Lobelia erinus*; and 'April Beauty' and 'White Triumphator' tulips. We pot up the tulips in the fall, heel them in over the winter, and put on our display in the bud stage. We also like 'Foxy' foxglove; we start the seeds in early fall and overwinter the seedlings in a heated cold frame. 'Good Hope' streptocarpella, a smaller and bushier cultivar of streptocarpus, is another favorite. For fall display we train the 'Bonsai' varieties of chrysanthemums from Sunnyslope Gardens to espalier on iron "trees."

Bud Heist
Owner, Heistaway Gardens, Conyers, Georgia

Many perennials will thrive in containers. My list of favorites is full of quick-blooming kinds that provide lots of color the first season, so that winter survival is not so important. These include:

Digitalis 'Excelsior'
Rudbeckia cultivars, which come in several heights
Coreopsis verticillata 'Moonbeam'
Echinacea purpurea (purple coneflower)
Lavendula latifolia (lavender)
Liatris spicata (gayfeather)
Verbascum chaixii 'Album'; blooms all summer
Verbena tenuisecta
Boltonia asteroides 'Snowbank'.

For shade, I prefer the following, all of which require more water than the first list. The cultivars I have starred look good in hanging baskets in partial shade.

Brunnera macrophylla (Siberian bugloss)
Myosotis scorpioides (forget-me-not), also sold as *M. palustris*
Lobelia cardinalis (cardinal flower), a good deep red
Lobelia siphilitica (blue cardinal flower)
Ceratostigma plumbaginoides (plumbago)

Not all herbaceous perennials will survive the winter here in containers. I consider these the most likely to survive if given good drainage and planted in large-enough containers:

Aurinia saxatilis (we still call it *Alyssum saxatile*)
Artemisia stellerana
Boltonia asteroides 'Snowbank'; grown for fall bloom
Cheiranthus cheiri (wallflower)
Dianthus plumarius (cottage pink)
Santolina chamaecyparissus (lavender cotton)

Sedum 'Autumn Joy', 'Indian Chief', 'Vera James'; for fall bloom
Macleaya cordata (plume poppy).

John Popenoe
Director, Fairchild Tropical Gardens, Miami

Because of the high maintenance requirements of most flowering plants, I use only drought-tolerant species such as the succulents and cycads for containers in southern Florida. The cycads do well for us. Although the thick-leaved types do best, as they are drought-resistant and slow-growing, *Dioon merolae* has proven satisfactory here. We seldom water these plants; they can almost get by on natural rainfall. *Asparagus sprengeri* is also a reliable performer and requires little care.

Joy Benton
Horticulturist, Longue Vue Center for Decorative Arts, New Orleans

The ixoras (Florida honeysuckle) are wonderful for color during our long, hot, humid growing season. We have several cultivars, including the common red, pink, and yellow and the newest, a dwarf red.

Seasonal favorites with visitors include streptocarpus (Cape primrose), yellow calla lilies, and lily-of-the-valley, a perennial that is little known here. It requires a long dormant period, which we can't provide, so we grow it yearly from pips. For winter color we grow calceolaria and cineraria in unheated greenhouses. Visitors like the beautiful, long-lasting wax begonia 'Avalanche' in pink and white, and the lily-flowered tulips, which we grow as annuals.

Jeanette Windham
Commercial landscape designer and contractor, Summerfield, North Carolina

Our winter climate is tremendously variable, and very few plants do well in containers all year here. The only ones I use anymore are conifers. Maintenance is low, and no winter protection is needed. I like to mix foliage colors, forms, and sizes in groups to create interest. My favorite conifers are all dwarf and slow-growing. I advise my clients to give their little conifers afternoon shade and plenty of water during the summer, but the plants are happy on sunny decks and patios in winter.

If your budget is limited, select plants from the *Pinus* or *Juniperus* genus, such as *Pinus thunbergiana* (Japanese black pine) and *Juniperus chinensis* 'Kaizuka'. Both of these look good in contemporary settings.

Large plants of the following slow-growing cultivars are rather expensive but highly desirable. Try *Chamaecyparis obtusa* (false cypress), including 'Nana Gracilis', which has pretty, fan-shaped green foliage; 'Mariesii', with gold tips; and 'Minima', a very slow-growing, very small cultivar. *Chamaecyparis pisifera* 'Aurea Nana' is a nice weeping yellow tree. All *Chamaecyparis* species may need to have the browning needles inside the plant pruned or shaken out in early spring to improve their appearance. Some winter burn may occur in full sun, but the plants always green up in the spring after they are fertilized with a balanced slow-release plant food.

Picea pungens 'Montgomery' is a compact plant with beautiful blue-gray new growth. Suitable *Tsuga canadensis* (hemlock) species include the weeping form, 'Sargentii'; 'Jedolah', which appears layered, with blue-green foliage; and 'Bennett's', which is faster-growing and weeps at the tips.

Taxus densiformis (yew) is great in northern exposures, but it doesn't like our summer sun. You can prune it to the desired shape. The Japanese yews are also good, but grow much more slowly.

Charles L. Ford IV
Superintendent of horticulture, Brookgreen Gardens, Murrells Inlet, South Carolina

Many of our container plants were given to us after they grew too large for home interiors and patios. We also propagate some of our own. Some are houseplant species, but we also have palms and citruses. Unusual ones that get lots of compliments are *Brugmansia insignis, Callitris preissii,* and *Cycas revoluta.* We protect these through the winter; our hardy species include variegated conifers, *Raphiolepis,* and crape myrtle. Even though it is deciduous, crape myrtle is very effective in winter when placed against a light-colored background.

MIDWEST

Inez Goodzey Berg
Director of horticulture, Washington Park Botanical Garden, Springfield, Illinois

Some of the most effective plants that we have used in containers include *Coleus* 'Hollywood Red' (grown from cuttings), *Pennisetum setaceum* 'Atrosanguineum' (purple fountain grass), and various crotons and oleanders. We often use *Vinca major* vines, *Begonia* 'Pink Avalanche', and *Asparagus sprengeri* as cascades to soften the edges of the containers.

Rachel Snyder
Editor (retired), *Flower & Garden*, Kansas City, Missouri

Some of the deciduous plants that we have used in permanent outdoor container landscapes are red-leaf barberry and 'Crimson Pygmy' barberry (*Berberis*), Washington hawthorns (*Crataegus*), various cultivars of honey locust (*Gleditsia triacanthos*), golden rain trees (*Koelreuteria paniculata*), shrub roses such as 'The Fairy', redbuds (*Cercis canadensis*), Callery pear cultivars such as 'Bradford', globe locusts (*Robinia pseudoacacia*), and cultivars of the seedless ash (*Fraxinus pennsylvanica*). We also like certain needle-leaved evergreens: *Juniperus chinensis* cultivars, such as 'Pfitzerana' and 'Armstrongii'; *Juniperus horizontalis* cultivars, such as 'Bar Harbor' and 'Plumosa' ('Andorra'); the compact forms of *mugo* pines; and the Colorado blue spruce (*Picea pungens*). The only broadleaf evergreens we have consistently used successfully to date are *Yucca filamentosa* and *Yucca glauca*.

W. Brian Ward
Horticulture superintendent, Missouri Botanical Garden, St. Louis

My favorites among the hundreds of cultivars we grow each year are *Verbena peruviana*, an excellent hanging-basket plant; *Acalypha hispida* (chenille plant), a novel and showy basket plant; the variegated St. Augustine grass (*Stenotaphrum secundatum* 'Varie-gatum'), which is very different from the general run of container plants; and *Coleus lanuginosus*, with eye-catching blue flowers, *Coleus blumei*, which makes a wonderfully vigorous basket plant, and *Coleus amboinicus*, which looks like a succulent and has highly pungent leaves. The cascading *Achimenes* 'Violet Night' makes a dramatic impact later in the season.

We give top marks to *Impatiens* 'Showstopper Pink'; it is the most compact and floriferous impatiens on the market. Here, in partial shade, fuchsias really shine. We grow them in our green-house during the winter and display them in hanging baskets outdoors during the summer. The 'Strap' series of variegated caladium cultivars are also great for growing in moderate shade.

We also like the warm colors of the old nasturtium variety 'Golden Gleam', which grows well here. We use *Mimulus* (mon-key flower) 'Freckle Face' for spring color, and we plug parsley, one of the best green foliage plants, into hanging baskets and among annual plants in freestanding containers.

We plunge containers of tender perennials into flower borders to restrict the root run and to make moving plants to the green-house in the fall an easier task. Pots make these plants bloom better and minimize the shock of transplanting and moving. We use this technique for *Lantana camara*, *Lantana montevidensis*, *Hibiscus rosa-sinensis* 'Variegata', *Gomphrena* (globe amaranth) 'Buddy', *Euryops athanasiae*, *Melampodium padulosum*, *Dyssodia tenuiloba*, *Caladium* cultivars, *Coleus* 'Duke's Yellow', *Calendula* cultivars, sweet basil 'Spicy Globe', pansy cultivars, and *Laurus nobilis* (bay) for summer growth in the scented garden.

Donald E. Slogar
Manager, Rockefeller Park Greenhouse, Cleveland

Some of our more successful container plant combinations are fibrous-rooted begonias and *Lobelia* 'Crystal Palace'; geraniums and 'Cascade' petunias with foliage-plant greens; *Dracena* with petunias or impatiens; different colors of cascading chrysanthe-mums in hanging baskets; and statice or impatiens with vinca vine or one of the ivies. For large containers, we group different summer annuals around a clump of dwarf cannas in a comple-mentary color.

We have come to rely on several flowers as dependable con-tainer and hanging-basket types: New Guinea and regular *Impa-tiens wallerana* hybrids, *Begonia* 'Angel Wing' cultivars, trailing jasmine, *Thunbergia* (clock vine), and verbena.

Matthew S. Rosen
Administrator, Des Moines Botanical Center, Des Moines

Tubs of tree-form hibiscus, lantana, and poinsettias give us ac-cents of seasonal color. During the summer, we display life-size topiary figures of horses, cows, turkeys, and chickens, and at Christmastime a topiary sled gets a lot of attention. Creeping fig is the plant we use to cover the topiary frames.

WEST AND SOUTHWEST

Judy L. Mielke
Senior horticulturist, Desert Botanical Garden, Phoenix

Most of our containers are planted with a single species, such as a clump of aloe or a specimen barrel cactus. A few of our planters have a combination of plants, arranged for variety in height, shape, and texture. For example, one of the shallow cast-concrete planters contains an ocotillo for height, two barrel cacti for mass, and the low, delicately textured forms of hedgehog and pincu-shion cacti as a ground cover.

My favorites among the succulents are the aloes. They offer a variety of shapes and colors, and spread by offsets to fill the container. Few of the succulents used elsewhere for hanging bas-kets will do well here, because of our summer heat, but *Sarcos-temma viminale* and *Stapelia* species are exceptions.

The annuals we have had the most success with are *Dyssodia tenuiloba* (golden fleece) and *Catharanthus roseus* (Madagascar periwinkle).

Lucy Tolmach
Garden superintendent, Filoli, Woodside, California

My favorites for containers are pelargoniums and geraniums grown from seeds, which last all season; *Cineraria* 'Sitters', for

March-April bloom in eight-inch pots; impatiens, which blooms all summer in moderate shade; and petunias, which we use principally for instant color for parties, as they are rather short-lived for us. *Narcissus* 'Golden Harvest' is a great cultivar for pots. We also use *Helichrysum petiolatum*, which we combine with seed-grown geraniums as the British do. Both dwarf citruses and Asiatic hybrid lilies are great for containers. One of our most novel uses of container plants involves the salmon-pink cultivar of canna lily, 'Los Angeles'. We grow it in fifteen-inch Spanish fern pots and place them in our pools for summer color.

Cecily Ring Gill
Horticulturist, Tucson Botanical Gardens, Tucson

We have been able to acquire and experiment with a number of flowering perennials and shrubs native to our desert and to similar climates elsewhere. Innovative nurserymen in our area have been most cooperative in scouting new prospects. Our large whiskey-barrel garden is a demonstration of flowering container plants that thrive in full desert sun at hundred-degree temperatures.

The prettiest flowers in the barrels are the 'Mount Lemmon' marigold (*Tagetes lemmonii*), a mass of yellow blooms in autumn. The desert rose mallow (*Pavonia lasiopetala*) gives us pink during the summer; it looks good with the ever-popular 'Blue Cape' plumbago. Visitors especially like our combinations of hybrid and native columbines grouped in barrels for early summer color.

Mark A. Dimmitt
Curator of plants, Arizona-Sonora Desert Museum, Tucson

One of the Desert Museum's goals is to introduce new plants suitable for cultivation in the desert climate. We have an active program for searching and testing. Our displays have helped to generate local demand, and some of these species are now carried by local nurseries, especially those with large collections of succulents.

Among my favorite container plants is *Adenium obesum*, also called Karoo rose, impala lily, or sabi star. A spectacular succulent from arid Africa that is well adapted to the desert, it also does well in other parts of the country that have long, hot summers; the plants don't mind high humidity. They must be brought in during cold weather, but can be kept in any frost-free place. I put mine in the garage from November to April, without light or water. The better clones bloom all year.

The small to medium-size species of agaves do well in containers and can be found in specialty nurseries. My favorites are *A. pelona*, *A. zebra*, *A. victoriae-reginae*, *A. ocahui*, *A. toumeyana* 'Bella', *A. parryi* 'Truncata', and *A. parryi* 'Compacta'. All of these are hardy to at least 15°F.

The native ocotillo (*Fouquieria splendens*) is sensitive to over-watering and grows very slowly, but the Mexican tree ocotillo (*F. macdougalii*) grows fast and does well in large containers. It also flowers three times a year, for a month or two each time. It is hardy to about 25°F and can be stored in darkness where winters are cold and long. Because it is native to a humid climate, it would probably perform well in the South. In cool zones of Southern California it grows slowly.

Elephant trees from the genera *Bursera*, *Operculicaria*, and *Pachycormus* have swollen trunks that make them very distinctive. *Bursera odorata*, also called *B. fagaroides* 'Elongata', has white bark and is especially attractive. Most species of these large shrubs are very tender to frost but can be stored in the dark for several months. *Pachycormus* is hardy to the mid-twenties. Most will probably grow in the Deep South.

Ficus petiolaris var. *palmeri*, the rock fig, is a very tender "strangler fig" that has adapted to the desert of Baja California, where it grows on rock cliffs instead of trees. Mount it on a decorative rock in a twelve-inch or larger container, and it will become a beautiful specimen in two to four years. It will grow very fast until it becomes rootbound, then it nearly stops, so its size is controlled by the size of the container.

We like to use cycads in containers here. Two relatively hardy species, *Cycas revoluta* and *Dioon edule*, will withstand our intense desert sun. *Encephalartos horridus* and *Zamia furfuracea* are excellent in partial shade but are tender to frost; both are beautiful.

We grow the kaffir lily (*Clivia miniata*) in very deep shade; the evergreen strap leaves are attractive all year. The flowers are stunning. Despite their leafiness, the plants don't require frequent watering.

The pincushion cacti (*Mammillaria* species) and hedgehog cacti (*Echinocereus* species) look great in pots, either singly when mature or grouped in large planters. The showy flowers of cacti are a bonus, for the spiny plants are attractive year round. Many are hardy to 20°F or lower, but they must not be overwatered.

Wade Roberts
Garden director, Sherman Library and Gardens, Corona del Mar, California

Our site on the Southern California coast provides such a mild climate that we have no need to protect plants from winter cold. *Streptocarpella* is an exception: we water it well and move it under a glass-covered porch to protect it from the cold. *Streptocarpella* 'Concord Blue' (known as 'Good Hope' on the East Coast) draws more attention than any other plant in our gardens. We set a six-inch plant in a fourteen-inch hanging basket, and with regular feedings and pinching it becomes a spectacular full-flowering basket in about six months. *Mandevilla splendens* 'Red Riding Hood' also makes a splendid, continuously blooming hanging basket for us.

Our "touch and smell" garden contains over fifty fragrant herbs in containers that are raised to waist level so that wheelchair-bound or blind visitors can reach out and touch them.

Walden R. Valen
Director, Strybing Arboretum and Botanical Gardens, San Francisco

In our largest containers we grow pine, birch, fir, podocarpus, and gingko trees, and wisteria. Smaller containers are used for seasonal annuals, and hanging baskets and wall baskets hold tuberous begonias and fuchsias.

Visitors most often praise our container plantings of blue *Salvia* 'Victoria', spring shows of tulips, anemones, and narcissi, and somewhat later shows of lilies. Everyone loves the lobelias, fuchsias, and tuberous begonias, which grow quite well here. Perhaps the greatest praise is received by our lavender 'Phoenicia' azaleas, which are trained to tree form and grown in five-gallon and fifteen-gallon planters.

. . . .

NORTHWEST

Jack Poff
Head gardener, Berry Botanic Garden, Portland, Oregon

Visitors seem to like the saxifragas and drabas grown in handmade replicas of early English stone troughs or sinks. My own favorites for containers are among the heaths: the prostrate gaultherias, the cassiopes, the andromedas, and kalmiopsis.

ZONE MAP

This map was compiled by the United States Department of Agriculture as a broad guideline to temperature extremes in your area. The key below gives you the average minimum temperatures of the ten zones. Determine if your area corresponds to its zone allocation by comparing your coldest temperatures with those given in the key.

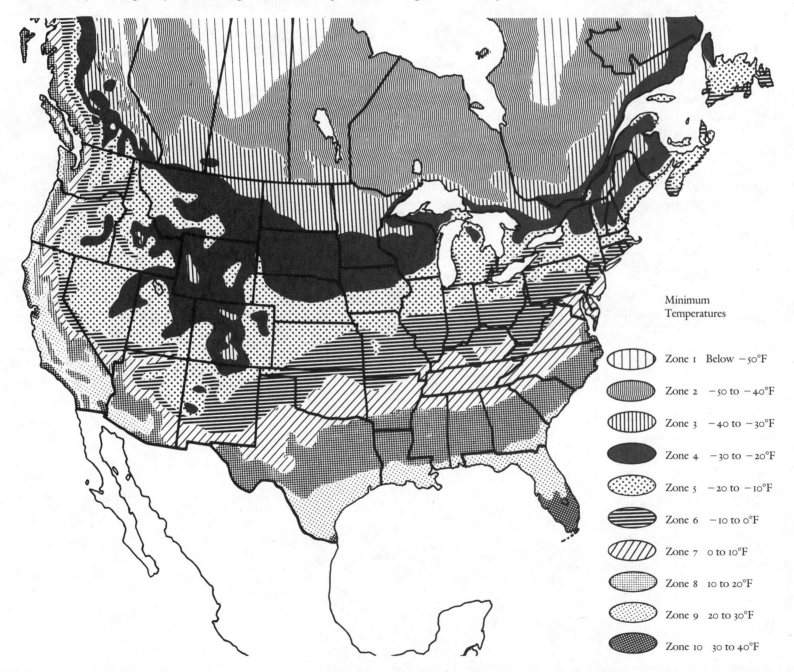

Minimum
Temperatures

Zone 1   Below −50°F

Zone 2   −50 to −40°F

Zone 3   −40 to −30°F

Zone 4   −30 to −20°F

Zone 5   −20 to −10°F

Zone 6   −10 to 0°F

Zone 7   0 to 10°F

Zone 8   10 to 20°F

Zone 9   20 to 30°F

Zone 10   30 to 40°F

Acknowledgments

Any married writer must have not just the tolerance of his spouse for the long hours of concentrated effort required to research and write a book, but her whole-hearted support, understanding, and, often, extra patience and forgiveness. Deadlines, real and self-imposed, require teamwork, clear telephone lines, a quiet house, and much errand-running. I have received all that and more from my wife, Jane, in addition to sound technical advice drawn from her background in biology, and I am pleased to dedicate this book to her.

A book such as this is difficult to write because it must be accurate and comprehensive yet easily comprehended by gardeners with middle-range skills. I prevailed on several friends in the nursery supply business and at botanical gardens across the country to help me check facts and review current practices. Fortunately, I had at Houghton Mifflin

Company a veteran editor, Frances Tenenbaum, who helped greatly in organizing the mass of material, and a skilled manuscript editor, Liz Duvall, who helped winnow the chaff from the wheat.

Special thanks go to my friends of many years Hollis M. Barron and Gerald Curtice. Hollis is a soil scientist; Jerry is a chemist who works with wetting agents and surfactants. They reviewed my copy on potting soils and planter mixes, plant foods, and watering. Shawn Delaney and Julio Navarro-Monzo, who formulate planter mixes and potting soils, also gave me good advice. I only hope that in simplifying and paraphrasing their detailed technical information, I have done justice to it.

Linda Yang, a fellow garden writer and landscape architect with special experience in rooftop and urban gardens, was a great help. Linda tried to prevail on me to extend my stated northern limits of hardiness of plants in containers, because she has seen many perennial plants, woody shrubs, and conifers survive in the New York City area. I waffled, feeling that urban warmth, winter watering, and oversize containers might explain these successes. Yet just before this book went to press, I visited a rooftop garden in downtown Chicago, which is in Zone 5; the good gardener there, Rosalind Reed, had a list of about two dozen perennials that lived for as long as seven years in containers with no protection. However, they were all species that are hardy in Zone 4.

A number of botanical gardens replied to a letter I sent asking for the·names of species and cultivars that perform well in their area and that seem to please visitors. They also sent me their recipes for soil mixes, so I had best explain why I have not published them. They are good mixes, but they are so varied, and in some cases so exotic, that I feared they would confuse gardeners. I urge you to refer to the appendix for the lists of plants these gardens sent, and to think about trying some of the plants recommended by botanical gardens in your region.

Botanical gardens are great places to see containers of all kinds. Usually cultivars are clearly labeled. I must say, though, that the most outstanding displays I have ever seen are at three of the regional Victory Gardens: the "home" garden on the grounds of Lexington Gardens in Lexington, Massachusetts; Victory Garden West, at Rogers Garden Center, Newport Beach, California; and Victory Garden South, at Callaway Gardens in Pine Mountain, Georgia. I am told that one container garden is even better, and I have

put it on my "must see" list: it beautifies the twenty-two acres of New York City's Rockefeller Center.

I would have been lost when it came to growing fruit trees in containers if it were not for the concise information contributed by Paul C. Stark of Stark Bros. Orchards and Nurseries, in Louisiana, Missouri, and by my old friend Don Dillon of Four Winds Growers, producers of dwarf citrus and avocado trees in Fremont, California.

My thanks to Mary Higgins of Centerville, Ohio, for showing me how she overwinters five dozen tender container plants on a twelve-by-fourteen-foot sunporch. I was amazed at the big plants she grew in relatively small containers: hibiscus, bougainvillea, lantana, and mandevilla, for example. Mary has grown over one hundred container plants for seven years, beginning when literature on the subject was scant and working out her own solutions to problems while building a showplace garden.

Jeanette Windham of Greensboro, North Carolina, a landscape designer, has utilized containers of choice dwarf conifers in her projects for many years. Jeanette gave me a great deal of valuable information on winter survival and ways to minimize winter injury to woody plants.

Everitt Miller, now retired from Longwood Gardens in Pennsylvania, contributed the historical information in the introduction.

Finally, my appreciation goes to the extension specialists in horticulture, entomology, and plant pathology at South Carolina's Clemson University, for patiently answering dozens of questions on matters that are too specific for this old generalist.

Index